T0267025

AFC WIMBLEDON

On This Day

AFC WIMBLEDON

On This Day

History, Facts & Figures from Every Day of the Year

GARY JORDAN AND STEPHEN CRABTREE

Foreword by Ian Cooke

First published by Pitch Publishing, 2022

Pitch Publishing
9 Donnington Park,
85 Birdham Road,
Chichester,
West Sussex,
PO20 7AJ
www.pitchpublishing.co.uk
info@pitchpublishing.co.uk

A CIP catalogue record is available for this book
from the British Library.

ISBN 978 1 80150 196 5

Typesetting and origination by Pitch Publishing
Printed and bound in Great Britain by TJ Books, Padstow

This book is dedicated to all the Wimbledon fans, players, staff and even those who watched the club rise through the years with some envy. It was, and still is, an incredible journey, and among these pages are some of the stories of what a small, unfashionable team in south-west London achieved against the odds.

Gary Jordan is a sportswriter for *The American* and has two published books, *Out of the Shadows: The Story of the 1982 England World Cup Team* and *Show Me the Way to Plough Lane: The Remarkable Story of Wimbledon's Return Home.* He is an AFC Wimbledon season ticket holder.

Stephen Crabtree was first taken to Plough Lane by his grandfather as a six-year-old in 1968 and has supported the Dons ever since. The author of several books about the club, he edits the fanzine *The Historical Don*, designed to celebrate all things yellow and blue.

Acknowledgements

When I first thought about compiling a book like this, telling the unique story of Wimbledon FC over the years through snapshots of their highs and lows, I realised it was a two-man job. There are a few worthy club historians who could have helped with this project, but the first one who came to mind was Stephen. An encyclopaedic knowledge is often read through his superb fanzine and the pictorial books he's self-published. So, of course, I was very pleased when he agreed to join me in co-writing this book. Alongside him and always helpful are the team at Pitch Publishing, from agreeing that this was something that was worthwhile to helping design the amazing cover you are holding right now – a big thank you to them. As always when writing it takes you away from everyday life, so I thank my family for their support and tolerance when I see the work coming along and get too excited! Lastly, thanks to Ian Cooke for writing the foreword, which sets the tone for the book.

Gary Jordan

Foreword by Ian Cooke

It is a great pleasure to be asked to write the foreword to this book of snapshots from Wimbledon's glorious history. Although I cannot claim to go back all the way to 1889, when the club was formed by old boys from the Central School near Wimbledon Common, having joined when the Dons were still an amateur side I have seen first-hand many of the matches and incidents remembered here.

I was only just out of my teens when I made my debut in an Isthmian League game at Kingstonian in April 1964, and for the next decade I was part of the Dons' Southern League side. I was approaching the veteran stage when Allen Batsford took over in the summer of 1974 and never in my wildest dreams could I have imagined what would happen next – captaining the team to three successive titles and those never-to-be-forgotten FA Cup ties against Burnley, Leeds and Middlesbrough.

I left as the club were elected to the Football League and I looked on with pride as my old team-mate Dave Bassett oversaw the amazing journey up through the divisions to the top flight. He left but the success continued with the 1988 FA Cup win and Wimbledon becoming founder members of the Premier League. Like every fan, I was outraged when the FA allowed the club to relocate up the M1, but we were ready to start again.

Beginning in the Combined Counties League in 2002, AFC Wimbledon have been on another remarkable journey that has included three titles and five promotions on the way back into the Football League. While the last decade has been more up and down, the greatest achievement of all has been securing an impressive new home on Plough Lane, just a Dickie Guy-length goal kick from where I played for all those years in the 1960s and 70s.

This is also the story of the men who have made the Dons great. 'Doc' Dowden and Harry Stannard, Roy Law and Eddie Reynolds, Jeff Bryant and Dickie Guy, Alan Cork and John Leslie, Nigel Winterburn and Dave Beasant, Robbie Earle and John Scales, Warren Barton and Marcus Gayle, Joe Sheerin and Matt Everard, Danny Kedwell and Jon Main, Barry Fuller and Lyle Taylor, right up to modern-day heroes like Jack Rudoni and Will Nightingale.

I hope that the memories this book brings back are as happy as mine.

Ian Cooke

305 goals in 609 appearances between 1964 and 1977

Introduction

Everyone will look back to certain points in life and particular dates that stand out as landmark moments. The day they overachieved at sports day, the day they broke an arm or leg, their first real date, kiss, and perhaps eventual marriage. Going on their first holiday abroad, buying their first car and moving out into their first home. All life-changing moments that will live long in the memory. This is not really different when it comes to sporting events, whether witnessed on television, or live in person at a stadium or arena. That feeling of euphoria at the last-minute winner, or the despair when you concede that penalty against your rivals. It sticks in your mind until the next time, the next big moment. Sometimes they don't just happen on the pitch. They may happen off it when a favoured player or manager leaves the club, or even worse, a boardroom split that sees the unimaginable occur.

These events may not be life-changing to everyone, some people will react differently in certain circumstances, but nevertheless they are still moments in time that need to be preserved and cherished. Over the years, Wimbledon Football Club has seen its fair share of highs. The club has always thrived on being the underdog, especially when it came of age during the 1970s with famous FA Cup runs where players became household names, and illustrious foes were knocked off their mighty perches. The flipside of this is that over time the fans have also had to fight for the very survival of the club, and stave off mergers and relocations, until of course one famous move was allowed to happen. Never to be beaten though, the underdogs prevailing again, the Wombles were not going to give up and from that terrible summer in 2002 the club was born again to tell new stories and create further historical moments.

We hope that in the coming pages you will be taken on a journey that raises your eyebrows and saddens your heart. You might remember the day you were there and recall that special date; others will be thrilled by the history being told. The outcome is the same – this is your club's history, and you should all be pleased to be part of it. Enjoy!

AFC WIMBLEDON

On This Day

JANUARY

1st January 1988

There was talk of European football in SW19 after a 2-1 victory over Derby County – the win was their fourth in a row over the holiday period – moved the Dons into the First Division's top five. With the score at 1-1 in the 61st minute, John Fashanu beat England goalkeeper Peter Shilton with surely the most powerful header ever seen at Plough Lane.

1st January 2005

Dave Anderson brought a breathalyser into training and tested nine of the players after a Ryman League Division One Hogmanay horror show against Whyteleafe the previous day. 'I thought they were drunk the way they played as we lost,' the manager said. 'I was quite impressed with them actually as all of them managed to outsmart the machine.'

2nd January 1978

A disastrous day trip to Swansea led to the resignation of Allen Batsford. Defender Dave Galvin was left behind when the team coach pulled out of an M4 service station after lunch and the reshuffled Dons put up limited resistance in losing 3-0 to the high-flying Swans. In the aftermath, the manager resigned, stating interference from his chairman Ron Noades had made his job impossible.

2nd January 2016

The Dons showed their determination to make 2016 a promotion year by winning 4-1 at Cambridge United thanks to goals from Paul Robinson, Jon Meades, Lyle Taylor and Ade Azeez. 'It doesn't get much better than that,' manager Neal Ardley said. 'In the second half there was only one team that was going to win. We were breathtaking.'

3rd January 2000

TV replays showed that Ben Thatcher had clearly elbowed Sunderland's Nicky Summerbee in the face during the build-up to the only goal as the Dons' 11th game without defeat at Selhurst Park ensured they began the new millennium seven points clear of the Premier League's relegation places. 'If my elbow caught him, I apologise. It was certainly unintentional,' the left-back commented.

3rd January 2004

Looking to reach Wembley, the Combined Counties League Dons put three goals past BAT Sports at Kingsmeadow. 'They are an impressively run club but there is no way in a million years they are going to win the FA Vase this year,' Sports boss Andy Leader claimed. 'There are far bigger and better teams around in the northern section and they will shortly have to face one of them.'

4th January 1975

The part-time Dons stunned the football world by becoming the first non-league team since the Second World War to win an FA Cup tie on a top-flight ground. Mick Mahon's 49th-minute strike and a series of fine saves by Dickie Guy helped the Southern Leaguers to win at First Division Burnley with home manager Jimmy Adamson saying, 'They are a most professional side.'

4th January 2014

Debutant Charlie Wyke lifted the mood among the travelling supporters by scoring one and making another as the Dons cruised to a 3-0 victory at Wycombe Wanderers. After seeing his side record their first League Two win in eight games, jubilant manager Neal Ardley said, 'Now we have to put together a run of performances like that, so we start to move up the table.'

5th January 2015

Two Steven Gerrard goals sent Liverpool through to the FA Cup fourth round after a 2-1 win over a spirited Dons side. 'They should be proud of their performance, but this was a chance for us,' Neal Ardley said as he reflected on Adebayo Akinfenwa's 36th-minute equaliser. 'If we had a bit more quality and nous, we could have got something out of the game.'

5th January 2019

Kwesi Appiah's 90th-minute winner secured the Dons a dramatic 3-2 FA Cup third-round victory at Fleetwood Town. 'It's fabulous for everyone concerned,' manager Wally Downes said afterwards. 'All that the club has ever done is make history all of the time from the moment the club was started again until today. Now we need to take this form into the league games, so we get out of trouble.'

6th January 1968

Nearly 10,000 fans inside Plough Lane saw the Southern League Dons lose 4-0 to Third Division Bristol Rovers in the FA Cup second round. Writing in the *Sunday Express*, Alan Hoby asked the question, 'Why did Wimbledon lose when they had 75 per cent of the possession and the best player on the pitch in Stuart Davies?' His answer, 'Defensive mistakes and mediocre finishing.'

6th January 2001

After a draw with lower-league Notts County in the FA Cup, more than 400 supporters staged a sit-down protest against the club's proposed move to Milton Keynes. 'It is becoming a mental thing,' substitute Gareth Ainsworth said as he tried to explain the team's poor home form. 'Selhurst [Park] is not our proper home. Plough Lane used to be a fortress for the club but this place lacks atmosphere.'

7th January 1961

Peter Kenchington was the toast of Plough Lane after his hat-trick had helped knock holders Tooting & Mitcham out of the Surrey Senior Cup. Watched by over 7,000 fans, the Dons produced their best football of the season to totally outclass their local rivals as they won 5-0. Had Eddie Reynolds had his shooting boots on, the hosts could have scored double figures.

7th January 1978

Dario Gradi's first game as manager saw the relegation-threatened Dons do well to hold promotion-chasing Brentford to a draw at Plough Lane. 'I'm going to put this club on a more professional basis,' the new boss told reporters afterwards. 'I'm looking to sign young players. I want to establish this as a club where young players can develop and grow.'

8th January 1994

Dean Holdsworth's hat-trick in a 3-0 FA Cup third-round demolition of Scunthorpe United took his tally to 13 as he responded to owner Sam Hammam's promise to kiss his backside if he totalled 20 by the end of the season. With his team still in both the cups and the top half of the Premier League, the former Brentford striker was coming closer to meeting the owner's cheeky challenge.

8th January 1997

Clinical finishes from Efan Ekoku and Øyvind Leonhardsen were enough to secure the Dons a 2-0 win at Bolton and a place in the League Cup semi-finals. 'I have always said that my primary ambition for this club is to get into Europe,' manager Joe Kinnear said. 'I would love to get to Wembley for a cup final. I went there three times as a player and won the lot. I would love to make it four as a manager.'

9th January 1954

Those calling for Harry Stannard to be dropped were made to look foolish as the veteran striker scored twice in the Dons' 4-1 Surrey Senior Cup victory at Woking. After 19 seasons and well over 200 goals for the club, the 37-year-old, known by his team-mates as 'the 'gaffer', belied his years by leading the line superbly at Kingfield.

9th January 1991

A diving header from Alan Cork deep in injury time proved to be the last FA Cup goal ever scored at the old Plough Lane. 'It was one of those special nights,' the striker later recalled of the evening the Dons beat Aston Villa. 'Miserable weather, floodlights that barely lit the pitch, but the place was alive. I never liked Selhurst Park. Plough Lane and nights like that – that's what Wimbledon was about.'

10th January 1987

Dave Bassett blasted his top-flight team despite seeing Lawrie Sanchez and Glyn Hodges score late goals to deny Second Division Sunderland an FA Cup victory at Plough Lane. 'We were rubbish,' the manager fumed. 'There isn't a real professional at the club. We deserved nothing. Half of them looked like they were on drugs – sleeping drugs!'

10th January 2004

Returning to the scene of their first ever game, AFC Wimbledon's run of 32 consecutive Combined Counties League victories came to a halt with a 2-2 draw at Sandhurst Town's Bottom Meadow. 'Giving away a two-goal lead is something you shouldn't do,' admitted striker Joe Sheerin. 'That was very frustrating, but we will pick ourselves up and try to go on another run.'

11th January 1977

Having defended for nearly an hour on a snow-covered Ayresome Park pitch, the Southern League Dons were knocked out of the FA Cup in a third-round replay when Middlesbrough winger David Armstrong went down under the challenge of Kevin Tilley. 'I played the ball as he passed me and Armstrong just dived over my foot,' the 18-year-old right-back claimed after the future England winger had picked himself up to score.

11th January 1994

A stunning strike from Sheffield Wednesday's Mark Bright, seven minutes from time, ended the Dons' hopes of reaching their first League Cup semi-final. Wimbledon had the better of the first half but went behind just after the break. When Dean Holdsworth levelled, it should have led to a glorious finale but former Palace striker Bright broke home hearts when he swivelled and fired the ball past Hans Segers from 25 yards.

12th January 1980

Nineteen-year-old Dave Beasant had a debut to forget when he let Blackpool winger Colin Morris's second-half shot through his legs and into the net for the winner in a Third Division match at Plough Lane. 'I just wanted the ground to open up and swallow me,' the goalkeeper remembered. Starting in August 1981, the giant custodian went on to complete seven seasons without missing a game and cemented his status as one of the club's all-time greats after lifting the FA Cup at Wembley.

12th January 1999

Just days after beating Derby County 2-1 to move into the Premier League's top six, the Dons broke their transfer record by signing John Hartson from West Ham for £7.5m. 'I'm delighted,' manager Joe Kinnear said. 'John is a smashing lad and a top-quality striker who has proved himself with 24 goals last season. We are building a squad here to take the club to the next level.'

13th January 1990

The Dons hustled champions Arsenal out of their stride to record a famous victory at Plough Lane. Defeat at WBA in the FA Cup the previous weekend had led manager Bobby Gould to drop Dennis Wise, Terry Gibson and Carlton Fairweather, which allowed debutant Mickey Bennett to score a late winner. 'I just got the ball and space opened up in the box which allowed me to shoot,' the former Charlton man said. 'It was a dream come true.'

13th January 2007

The Dons stunned the full-time professionals of Conference National side Gravesend & Northfleet with an FA Trophy win at Stonebridge Road. The Ryman Leaguers took the lead 11 minutes after the interval through Roscoe D'Sane, and such was the quality of their back four, marshalled by Paul Lorraine, that Andy Little was largely untested in goal from then on.

14th January 1950

Appearing live on BBC TV for the first time in their history, the Dons, eagerly awaited FA Amateur Cup meeting with local rivals Kingstonian at Richmond Road was a disappointing spectacle. 'Nerves were only to be expected in such an important cup game but there is no doubt that the biggest factor in unsettling the players was the thought of television cameras following their every move,' wrote one of the local press reporters after two goals from Ron Head had given Wimbledon victory.

14th January 1995

'He's Efan sent!' trumpeted one newspaper headline as ex-Canary Efan Ekoku grabbed the winner in the Dons' 2-1 victory at Norwich. 'It makes really nice reading to see Wimbledon seventh in the Premiership,' manager Joe Kinnear said. 'The ambition is to finish higher than the sixth place we managed last season and get into Europe. When we sold John Fashanu and John Scales everyone had us down as relegation candidates, so it just shows you write us off at your cost.'

15th January 1949

With the prospect of a Wembley final for the first time, there was excitement in the air as the Dons hosted Salisbury City in the first round of the FA Amateur Cup. With Plough Lane still showing signs of war damage, a large crowd watched the hosts win 2-1 thanks to a late goal from Freddie Gauntlett. There was real disappointment when eventual winners Bromley eliminated them in front of a record Hayes Lane crowd of 10,649 in round two.

15th January 1966

Goals from Dave Peters and Eddie Reynolds saw the Dons beat a star-studded Worcester City outfit and keep the pressure on leaders Weymouth at the top of the Southern League. The matchday programme bemoaned the fact that some fans had been throwing stones from the open east terrace at the windows of nearby buildings causing damage and, it was stated, 'Unless it stops the club will be impelled to take action against the culprits.'

16th January 1999

Booed every time he touched the ball at White Hart Lane, debutant John Hartson ensured that the Tottenham defence were given a bruising afternoon as the Dons secured a Premier League draw. Most of the post-match controversy concerned David Ginola with Spurs saying he should have had four penalties and the visitors claiming he had repeatedly dived. 'Ten out of ten to the referee,' manager Joe Kinnear said. 'He was very brave.'

16th January 2021

Former loan striker Charlie Wyke returned in the colours of Sunderland to score a hat-trick and condemn the Dons to the relegation places after their fourth League One defeat in a row. 'I changed the formation three times today in the game,' manager Glyn Hodges said. 'We are trying everything to get out of this run. We know that the same players started the season fantastically and got points on the board. We are trying to help them and help each other.'

17th January 1970

It was the start of seven and a half unbroken seasons between the Wimbledon posts. As Southern League champions Cambridge United gained revenge for a defeat at Plough Lane two weeks earlier by winning the return 2-1, Dickie Guy was beginning a run of 312 consecutive Southern League games for the Dons that was only broken when the club joined the Football League in 1977.

17th January 2004

Missed chances and poor concentration saw the Dons blow a Wembley chance as they exited the FA Vase at the hands of a physical Colne side. Trailing 2-1 at the break, there could have been goals at both ends in an exciting second period, but the visitors held on. 'Everyone is disappointed with themselves,' midfielder Danny Oakins admitted afterwards. 'We let ourselves down by being far too relaxed at the start.'

18th January 1947

Led by the mayor of Wimbledon, councillor Cyril Black, more than 300 Dons fans travelled to the south coast to see their team beat Eastbourne 4-2 in the FA Amateur Cup first round. With just under 4,000 supporters inside The Saffrons at kick-off, a second-half double from Pat Edleston proved crucial as Wimbledon began a journey that was to take them all the way to the final. In the evening, the mayor hosted a dinner in honour of both participating teams.

18th January 1992

Clive Allen's second-half winner for Chelsea signalled the end of Peter Withe's disastrous managerial reign. Following just one win in 17 games and an alarming slide down the Premier League table, a board meeting the following Monday confirmed the inevitable as the Merseysider was replaced with reserve-team coach Joe Kinnear. The former Tottenham Hotspur full-back was put in temporary charge with a brief to save the club from relegation.

19th January 1991

A late free kick from the impressive Warren Barton was enough for the Dons to gain a point at Anfield. The visitors thoroughly deserved to draw after weathering a welter of Liverpool attacks, and the loss of John Fashanu through injury, before attacking on the break in the final half an hour. 'I didn't think about it at all,' Barton commented. 'Terry Gibson told me to keep the shot low and hard. So, I looked at the Kop, took a deep breath and hammered it.'

19th January 2010

Dogged defending, clinical finishing and generous refereeing all played a part as Wimbledon booked their place in the third round of the FA Trophy at the expense of unlucky Altrincham. Ricky Wellard had put the Dons ahead before, in the 41st minute, goalkeeper Seb Brown came racing out of his goal and sent Chris Senior flying. The referee only showed a yellow card and Wimbledon took advantage by going on to win 3-1.

20th January 2001

Constant rumours about the imminent sale of John Hartson seemed to unsettle the Dons as they lost 2-1 at Portsmouth to dent their hopes of an immediate return to the Premier League. 'John has never said he wants to move but the financial situation at the club means that it will happen,' frustrated manager Terry Burton said. 'I want to improve my squad, but it is difficult when I have to reduce the wage bill by £4m.'

20th January 2018

Joe Pigott scored on his debut as the Dons beat Blackpool 2-0 to move out of the League One relegation zone. Liam Trotter got the breakthrough for the hosts after the break before Pigott, signed from Maidstone in the week, sealed matters with 13 minutes remaining. 'Joe has played in the Football League before,' manager Neal Ardley said. 'We believe he has the potential to make a name for himself at this level.'

21st January 1961

Backed by more than 1,000 fans at Loakes Park, the Dons advanced into the second round of the FA Amateur Cup after a superb display produced their first win at Wycombe since 1950. Eddie Reynolds equalised the Wanderers' early goal just before half-time and when Norman Williams was left unmarked from a Peter Kenchington pass late on, he settled the match with a low drive.

21st January 2012

Jack Midson bagged a late double as the Dons twice fought back from being two goals down to grab a sensational 4-3 League Two victory at Gillingham. 'It is not often you come to a side in the play-off places, give them a two-goal start and win,' manager Terry Brown said. 'More than 1,000 of our fans have seen probably the most exciting game in AFC Wimbledon history today.'

22nd January 1972

The Dons were booed off the pitch after losing an FA Trophy match 5-1 at home to fellow Southern Leaguers Yeovil Town. 'I don't like making excuses, but you don't win cup ties without fighters – 11 fighters – and we were carrying about four passengers today,' manager Mike Everitt said in response to calls for him to be sacked. 'I don't mind a player having a bad game – we all do – as long as he gives 100 per cent.'

22nd January 2000

Goals from Robbie Earle and Marcus Gayle ensured the Dons beat Newcastle United and moved above the Geordies in the Premier League table. Two surveys of the top flight were published in the week that followed. The first found that Wimbledon supporters were the least racist in the division. The other showed that the Dons were the team most likely to be harshly treated by match officials. Only 35 per cent of decisions went in their favour compared to 87 per cent for Manchester United.

23rd January 1960

Nine coaches of travelling fans were left aggrieved as two debatable penalty decisions and a disallowed goal at Hendon put paid to the Dons' FA Amateur Cup ambitions for another year. On a quagmire of a pitch at Claremont Road, Norman Williams had a goal cancelled out for offside and the referee awarded a pair of spot-kicks that allowed Northern Ireland amateur international striker Jimmy Quail to score twice as the hosts won a hard-fought game 2-1.

23rd January 2016

The Dons extended their unbeaten run away from Kingsmeadow to eight matches and moved into the League Two play-off positions with an impressive 2-0 win at Notts County. 'We were outstanding from start to finish,' said manager Neal Ardley. 'To come here and have 18 attempts on goal – if we had won 4-0 it would not have been a story. We dominated them from start to finish and it is as complete an away performance as you will ever get.'

24th January 1981

The Wimbledon fans who had travelled to an FA Cup fourth-round tie at Wrexham protested over news of a proposed merger with Crystal Palace. With their team defeated 2-1, the supporters wanted guarantees about the long-term future of the club in the wake of chairman Ron Noades buying a controlling interest at Selhurst Park. When the dust settled, Sam Hammam took charge at Plough Lane and installed Dave Bassett as his manager.

24th January 1998

Despite both Robbie Earle and Ceri Hughes going off in the first ten minutes, a Neal Ardley goal proved enough for the Dons to emerge victorious from a tricky FA Cup fourth-round trip to Huddersfield Town. 'I thought our world was caving in,' manager Joe Kinnear said of the early injuries, and he revealed that Ardley had taken a knock as well. 'I was going to take him off too, but he wanted to play on, and he went on to score the winner.'

25th January 1975

Dickie Guy earned legendary status by saving Scottish international Peter Lorimer's late penalty to secure the Southern League Dons an FA Cup replay at First Division champions Leeds United. The bearded custodian made a string of fine saves as the hosts piled on the second-half pressure before the man with supposedly the hardest shot in football put his tame effort to the right of the goal and the London Docks tally clerk got down to push the ball away.

25th January 2011

Dominant during the first 45 minutes of a midweek visit to Bath City, the Dons were eventually relieved to escape Twerton Park with a Blue Square Premier point after the tables were turned in the second period. 'If you're top of any league and you're two goals up at half-time – whoever you are playing – you'd hope to see it out,' frustrated manager Terry Brown commented at the end.

26th January 1993

A record-low top-flight crowd shivered in the cold as the Dons slipped to a home Premier League defeat against Everton. 'How we escaped without being at least four down at half-time I will never know,' Toffees boss Howard Kendall said after seeing his side score three times after the interval. With just 3,039 fans inside Selhurst Park, it was hardly the 'whole new ball game' that the promoters had used to hype the new competition when it was launched the previous summer.

26th January 2008

With star striker Jon Main being stretched off in the second half, the Dons' hopes of landing the Ryman League title were left hanging by a thread after Tonbridge Angels hit back from two down to grab a point at Kingsmeadow. 'Draws at this stage are little better than losses and to throw away a two-goal lead was disappointing,' manager Terry Brown reflected. 'Jon will be out for a minimum of seven or eight weeks – it is a major blow.'

27th January 2001

Finally settling their FA Cup replay with Notts County at the third time of asking, a Trond Andersen goal deep in extra time took the Dons through to face Middlesbrough in round four. After a 2-2 draw at Selhurst Park, the first attempt at a replay was abandoned due to thick fog soon after half-time and the second never started because of a waterlogged pitch. 'It looked like the game was going to penalties, but Trond's header was a worthy winner,' manager Terry Burton said.

27th January 2018

By winning 4-0 at Valley Parade, the Dons completed an impressive double over Bradford City and moved four points clear of the League One relegation zone. A Cody McDonald double along with goals from Jimmy Abdou and Andy Barcham condemned the play-off-chasing Bantams to a humiliating defeat. 'We've had loads of games when we could have scored four or five, but have only scored one,' manager Neal Ardley said. 'Today, we had four or five chances and scored four.'

28th January 1989

FA Cup holders Wimbledon came through a tough examination to win a hard-fought fourth-round tie at Villa Park. A Vinnie Jones goal on the hour was enough to separate the sides but the visitors had Hans Segers to thank for a series of saves including a second-half penalty. 'We worked hard to win the cup in May and today proved that we will work just as hard to keep it,' manager Bobby Gould said at the end.

28th January 2012

If successive wins over Port Vale, Gillingham and Macclesfield Town had led many fans to believe Terry Brown's side had turned the corner after a dismal run of League Two results, the visit of Aldershot was a wake-up call. Two goals from Anthony Straker were enough for Dean Holdsworth's men to win 2-1 at Kingsmeadow to leave the Dons still dangerously close to the relegation places.

29th January 1955

An extra-time goal from Freddie Gauntlett saw the Dons beat Shildon 2-1 to advance into the third round of the FA Amateur Cup. A week earlier, Wimbledon had done well to return from facing the Durham Colliery side on a snow-covered pitch in the north-east with a replay. Having been entertained after the first game, home supporters laid on an after-match meal for the travelling fans who had made the journey south.

29th January 1982

Any euphoria following the struggling Dons' 3-1 Third Division win at Doncaster was tempered by the news that Dave Clement had broken his leg. 'I want to play for as long as possible, so I look on this as a little setback,' the 34-year-old former England right-back said in the week that followed. A month or so later, unable to contemplate not being able to play again, Clement took his own life.

30th January 1985

An early Paul Fishenden goal was enough to beat Nottingham Forest and take the Dons through to the FA Cup fifth-round for the first time in their history. 'We showed great spirit,' manager Dave Bassett commented at the end. 'We are a blood and guts team, and we go for the jugular. I don't care if people criticise our play. We are not a dirty team, but we do seem to scare some opposition sides.'

30th January 2021

Glyn Hodges was sacked after a dismal run of results had left the Dons deep in the relegation mire. 'It is with a genuinely heavy heart that I have to announce that we have parted company with Glyn,' CEO Joe Palmer announced. 'After a strong start to the season when the team was arguably over-performing, the recent run of results left us in a difficult position. We need to do everything to ensure our survival in League One.'

31st January 1981

Dave Bassett's first match in charge saw the Dons throw caution as they won a thrilling Fourth Division encounter 3-2 at Port Vale. 'It could not have gone any better,' the new boss enthused. 'We attacked, we entertained, and we scored goals. We also won and it is really satisfying when all those things go together. We've got an outside chance of going up, but we cannot afford any slip-ups.'

31st January 2009

With several hundred fans locked out, a record 4,690 crowd inside Kingsmeadow watched the Dons win the eagerly awaited top-of-the-table Conference South clash against Chelmsford City. Two clinical strikes from Jon Main put the hosts in control at half-time before Kevin James pulled one back to set up a nervy finale. Victory was finally secured by Tom Davis's late goal and left Wimbledon three points clear of the Essex Clarets with a game in hand.

AFC WIMBLEDON
On This Day

FEBRUARY

1st February 2011

The Dons' heavy schedule looked likely to derail their Blue Square Premier promotion hopes as they lost heavily at York City. 'It finally got to us – it was too much of an ask,' manager Terry Brown said. 'We have done 2,000 miles recently. It was too much to hope that we could win there after trips to Darlington, Bath, Fleetwood and Gateshead. York were the better side and scored three great goals.'

1st February 2020

Despite Joe Pigott's 73rd-minute goal, ten-man Accrington secured a vital 2-1 win over the relegation-threatened Dons. 'Them having a man sent off helped us make a fist of it, but I was really disappointed with the performance and the way we went about it,' manager Glyn Hodges said. 'It was probably the worst display in the 14 months since I've been back here. We could have maybe nicked something, but the quality wasn't there today.'

2nd February 1976

Two first-half goals at Victoria Park extinguished the desperately disappointed Dons' Wembley hopes for another year. 'We were diabolical and deserved to go out,' manager Allen Batsford said as he reflected on an FA Trophy defeat at Isthmian League Dagenham. 'We still have the Southern League and Southern League Cup to go for so we can make it a good season.'

2nd February 2008

The Ryman League Dons crashed out of the FA Trophy, beaten 2-0 by a Torquay United side challenging for a place back in the Football League. 'We've paid the price for progressing in the FA Trophy – too many injuries, too many suspensions and too many matches to fit in,' said manager Terry Brown. 'We now need to focus on winning promotion and on Monday I am going to speak to the chairman to see if I can go and get one or two players in.'

3rd February 1951

Harry Stannard scored what proved to be the winner as more than 8,000 fans saw the Dons do just enough to edge out Woking 3-2 in an FA Amateur Cup second-round tie. The huge public interest in the competition back then was shown by the fact that the four-game, third-round marathon against local rivals Tooting & Mitcham United that followed was watched by a total of over 42,000 fans.

3rd February 2002

Dons fans were unsure whether to cheer their favourites' 2-0 victory over runaway First Division leaders Manchester City or hold up signs to those watching on ITV stating 'Koppel Out'. Feelings were running high in the wake of a Football Association arbitration panel ruling that the Football League should re-examine the directors' case for moving the club to Milton Keynes.

4th February 1984

Alan Cork and the recalled Dean Thomas both scored twice as Third Division Wimbledon went on the rampage in east London. Mid-table Leyton Orient could not live with the free-flowing Dons who scored three in each half to end up as 6-2 winners. With the race for promotion to the Second Division beginning to hot up, the year of George Orwell's nightmare novel was to turn into a dream for Dave Bassett's men.

4th February 1997

A Marcus Gayle goal, scored from a close-range header in the 63rd minute, was enough to give the Dons an FA Cup fourth-round replay victory over holders Manchester United at Selhurst Park. Neil Sullivan made a series of fine saves as Joe Kinnear's men protected their lead in the final minutes. 'I have a hell of a lot of respect for them,' United boss Alex Ferguson commented afterwards. 'They are one of the best sides we've played all season.'

5th February 2005

The travelling supporters sang, 'Jesus Christ. Superstar. Signed from Dulwich on a free transfer!' at long-haired striker Andrew Martin as the Dons were held to a Ryman League Division One draw at Leatherhead. 'We knew it would be a hard game as they had won five on the trot,' assistant manager Jon Turner said. 'It was a very even match – I thought we shaded the first half, and they were better in the second.'

5th February 2021

Interim manager Mark Robinson saw his Dons side move out of the League One relegation zone with their first win in 12 matches after a 3-2 victory at fellow strugglers Wigan. 'The players can enjoy the moment, but by the time it gets to Sunday at 9pm I expect them to be looking ahead to Monday,' Robbo said. 'For 35 minutes, I felt we were close to where I want us to be if I get the opportunity, but you have to enjoy winning.'

6th February 1988

With the FA Cup fifth-round draw the previous Monday pairing the two sides together, it was inevitable that a First Division match between Wimbledon and Newcastle United should end in goalless stalemate with neither team prepared to risk going for the kill. Post-match, a picture of a snarling Vinnie Jones squeezing Paul Gascoigne's crown jewels went around the world and confirmed many of the prejudices people held about the Dons and their approach to the game.

6th February 1993

Capping a tremendous seven days in which they had won at Coventry and knocked Aston Villa out of the FA Cup, the Dons beat reigning champions Leeds United 1-0 at Selhurst Park. 'It's been a magnificent week,' manager Joe Kinnear commented after Dean Holdsworth's goal had separated the teams. 'The players have flogged themselves to death and got their reward. Looking at the two sides out there, we looked more like the champions than they did.'

7th February 2006

A goal scored five minutes into injury time ensured the Ryman League Dons held table-topping Braintree Town to a draw at Kingsmeadow. Future Don Paul Lorraine had headed what everyone thought would be the winner in the 90th minute but when the referee signalled seven minutes of added time a great roar went up around the ground. A spell of sustained pressure culminated in a free kick falling to Steve Butler who gleefully hit the equaliser into the roof of the net.

7th February 2015

Neal Ardley refused to criticise Adebayo Akinfenwa after he missed
the chance of a hat-trick with a casual penalty in the 2-0 League
Two home victory over Newport. 'I wouldn't have a pop at Adebayo,
he's too big,' the manager joked. 'He could have made life easier, but
strikers don't mean to miss goals. He has now been involved in 20
of our 40 goals this season so don't think that I'm going to have a
go at him when he doesn't get one of them right.'

8th February 1977

With over half of their Southern League matches to fit into the
final 14 weeks of the campaign, the Dons began their daunting
programme by beating high-flying Redditch in SW19. Surprise
title contenders, the Midlands side were undone by winger Barry
Friend whose crosses led Wimbledon to a 3-0 win. By the time of
the reverse fixture in May, Allen Batsford's team were hoping to
secure a third successive title to make their case for being elected
to the Football League unanswerable.

8th February 1992

Joe Kinnear was able to celebrate his first full week in charge
with a win after Terry Phelan's late strike secured a 2-0 victory
over Aston Villa at Selhurst Park. 'It was important the bubble
didn't burst after our display at Queens Park Rangers last week,'
the manager said. 'It hasn't surprised me how quickly things have
turned around. All I've done is cut down training to one day a week
and we spend the rest of the time in the pub!'

9th February 1998

'Marauding guests reduce Palace to rubble' ran the headline in *The
Times* after the Dons' first win since early December had lifted
them clear of the Premier League's bottom three. Two-goal Carl
Leaburn was the hero but with fans protesting over a planned move
to Dublin, manager Joe Kinnear was not in a good mood. 'The
demonstrations are a bit of a liberty,' he said. 'They should aim
their abuse at Merton Council. Other clubs get help with building
new stadiums, we just get custard pie in our faces. Sooner or later,
we will go down.'

9th February 2019

The League One relegation trapdoor seemed to be creaking open as the Dons lost 2-0 at home to Burton Albion. 'We've got to put performances in that motivate the fans,' manager Wally Downes said. 'The players have got to give the fans something to shout about. They at least want a team that is battling and fighting and today they didn't do that. They have got to dig themselves out of this hole and today we didn't do any digging.'

10th February 1975

Having dominated the back pages for days, over 45,000 fans turned out to watch the Southern League Dons' FA Cup replay with Leeds United. 'I thought Wimbledon played extremely well, particularly at the back,' Leeds boss Jimmy Armfield said after his side had won thanks to a deflected goal. 'They kept it so tight that our forwards were given little chance up front. David Harvey pulled off a couple of good early saves otherwise Wimbledon would have taken the lead.'

10th February 2007

Reeling from the news that the club had been deducted 18 points for fielding an ineligible player, the Dons nonetheless produced an outstanding performance in beating Bromley 3-2. 'The verdict is ridiculous,' manager Dave Anderson said. 'The decision tells me all I need to know about the people who run the FA and the Ryman League. We have 15 games left and if we won all of them that would take us up to 78 points. Not even Real Madrid could come back from this and make the play-offs.'

11th February 1995

Despite taking an early lead, the Dons crashed to their record Premier League defeat after conceding seven at Villa Park. Lying in ninth place having won four of their seven games since Boxing Day, the Wimbledon defence were nonetheless unable to prevent a deluge of goals. 'I feel totally and utterly embarrassed,' defender Andy Thorn said. 'We just were not at the races. Every part of our game was wrong. We got trounced and deserved it.'

11th February 2017

Tom Elliott scored a dramatic equaliser with the last kick of the game before being shown a second yellow card for over-celebrating as the Dons drew 1-1 with Charlton Athletic in an ill-tempered derby at Kingsmeadow. There was further controversy as a coin thrown from the away section hit the assistant referee and a Wimbledon volunteer abused Addicks boss Karl Robinson as he left the field at the end of the game.

12th February 1980

A 65th-minute John Leslie goal was enough for the Dons to beat ten-man Gillingham and raise hopes of avoiding relegation from the Third Division. 'It was important not to lose this one,' manager Dario Gradi commented. 'I did not have to say anything to my players before the game – they were straining at the leash after winning at Brentford on Saturday. With five points from the last six [three games, two points for a win] I am much happier with our position now.'

12th February 1994

John Fashanu headed the pick of the goals as the Dons put Kevin Keegan's expensively assembled Newcastle United team to the sword with a 4-2 win at Selhurst Park. 'It was a magnificent all-round performance – our best of the season,' manager Joe Kinnear said. 'We were always the governors today; we bossed the game. It is not a question of us surviving in the Premiership – I've always been confident we would stay up. But we've had to work hard to preserve our status.'

13th February 2001

An off-the-ball incident in the 76th minute involving Mark Williams and Middlesbrough's Ugo Ehiogu turned an FA Cup fourth-round replay in the Dons' favour. Neal Ardley levelled from the resulting spot kick before Wimbledon won the tie in extra time. 'My nose has been broken five times before, so he hasn't done any more damage,' Williams said of Ehiogu's dismissal. 'I've had a few elbows in my time but Ehiogu just turned and hit me straight in the face.'

13th February 2016

Lyle Taylor bagged two goals as the Dons equalled their biggest win of the season with a thumping 4-1 victory over Luton Town. 'It was very pleasing,' manager Neal Ardley said of a victory that lifted his side to tenth place in the League Two table, three points off the play-offs. 'We're trying to keep the players fresh, so we enjoy the last third of the season. We know that on our day we are as good as anyone, but we need to be consistent.'

14th February 1959

A come-from-behind victory allowed the Dons to beat Ilford 2-1 and move level on points with leaders Wycombe Wanderers at the top of the Isthmian League table. Chasing the game with 20 minutes to go, midfielder Geoff Hamm set up Norman Williams for the equaliser before scoring the winner himself with just minutes left.

14th February 2004

Just days after Terry Eames had been sacked for what the club described as 'gross misconduct', a hat-trick from Kevin Cooper and two apiece from both Ryan Gray and Gavin Bolger helped the Dons produce a 9-0 win at bottom-of-the-table Chessington United. 'It was really pleasing to see that the players didn't take outside events on to the pitch,' interim boss Nick English commented as the team's 25th win in 26 Combined Counties League matches kept them on course for the title.

15th February 1983

Mick Smith and Glyn Hodges were on target as the Dons beat Colchester United 2-1 to keep up their chase for the Fourth Division title. 'It depends on what you mean by attractive football,' manager Dave Bassett said in response to those who criticised his team's style of play. 'There is more goalmouth incident in our games than with lots of the other teams I have seen this season. Call it what you like – we are here to win games and get promotion.'

15th February 1997

Goals from Marcus Gayle and Robbie Earle were enough for the Dons to beat QPR 2-1 and move into the FA Cup quarter-finals. 'I missed the boat when we were 100-1,' manager Joe Kinnear said when asked about his side's new status as cup favourites. 'The [League Cup semi-final first leg] game on Tuesday at Leicester is the biggest game of the year and if we can get any type of result, we can bring them back here believing we have a chance of making it to Wembley.'

16th February 1963

Finally playing again after a near two-month break caused by the winter freeze, the Dons won 3-0 at Athenian League Southall in an FA Amateur Cup first-round replay. Having changed at the nearby Featherstone Road School due to burst pipes at the Western Road ground, the Wimbledon players adapted well to the muddy conditions and took control with two goals either side of half-time from Eddie Reynolds. It was the first step towards what fans hoped would be Wembley glory.

16th February 1999

A suspiciously offside-looking Steffen Iversen scored the only goal as the Dons missed out on a trip to Wembley after being beaten by Tottenham Hotspur in a League Cup semi-final second leg at Selhurst Park. Wimbledon threw everything at the north Londoners during a frantic second period and were unlucky not to force extra time as Robbie Earle, Marcus Gayle and Efan Ekoku all went close with long shots. But it was not Wimbledon's night.

17th February 1962

Wycombe coach Graham Adams slated the Dons' negative approach after his side had lost an FA Amateur Cup third-round tie watched by over 9,000 fans at Plough Lane. 'I give Wimbledon no credit for their win,' the former Plymouth player was quoted as saying. 'If they had played as they had started it would have been a great game, but I was disappointed to see them resorting to destructive tactics after they took that early lead.'

17th February 1996

Efan Ekoku's injury-time equaliser secured the Premier League Dons an FA Cup fifth-round replay against Huddersfield Town. 'A lot of teams would have faded after going two down, but my players stuck in there and Efan's come up trumps,' a beaming Joe Kinnear told the press. 'I thought the lads were magnificent in the way they kept going but I thought that we were not going to get the break we deserved.'

18th February 1984

The Dons missed the chance to go top of the Third Division after they were held to a 1-1 draw by lowly Scunthorpe United at Plough Lane. 'They were nervous, but we've got to learn to live with the pressure,' manager Dave Bassett said. 'We've lost some of our sparkle and if we want to win promotion we've got to get back to winning ways in a hurry. We're getting pretty tense before games now as we realise how close we are to success.'

18th February 1989

Backed by around 7,000 fans waving inflatable haddocks, Fourth Division strugglers Grimsby Town dominated an FA Cup fifth-round tie at Plough Lane for nearly an hour before the intervention of Dennis Wise changed the game. The tricky winger set up two goals and scored the third himself as the holders won through to a quarter-final at Everton. Grimsby's Keith Alexander mocked the hosts' reputation as hardmen afterwards. 'They are not half as tough as Scarborough or Lincoln,' he said.

19th February 1995

Robbie Earle hit a post with just minutes to go as the Dons drew an FA Cup fifth-round tie at Anfield. 'Our front two [Andy Clarke and Efan Ekoku] frightened the life out of them early on,' manager Joe Kinnear claimed. 'Robbie could have won it for us with that late chance but that would have been hard on Liverpool. It was a case of getting our pride back after losing 7-1 at Villa and I thought we caused Liverpool plenty of problems. We will give our usual 100 per cent in the replay.'

19th February 2019

Joe Pigott scored a hat-trick as AFC Wimbledon breathed life into their League One survival fight with a dramatic 4-3 win at relegation rivals Rochdale. 'It was a game beforehand that we said we had to win,' manager Wally Downes commented. 'I said at the weekend that we had 14 cup finals left and we had to win tonight, and we went out and did it. I was really pleased with the way we went forward trying to get the winner after we let them back in with that silly goal.'

20th February 1988

Silencing a hostile home crowd, the Dons won 3-1 at Newcastle to advance into the FA Cup quarter-final. 'We want to win the cup,' Lawrie Sanchez explained. 'If you went by what you read in the papers at the start of the season there would have been little point in us turning up for matches. According to some we were already relegated. They seem to forget we do not throw in the towel at Wimbledon.'

20th February 2010

A brilliant solo goal from Danny Kedwell sealed a 2-1 win at Luton Town and lifted the Dons back into the Blue Square Premier's top ten. 'They did what we aim to do away from home,' Hatters boss Richard Money commented. 'They defended really well, and they stuck their bodies in the way. Wimbledon are one of the strongest sides in the division and in Danny Kedwell they have a real gem.'

21st February 1930

Goals from Frank Okin, Harry Hopkins and 'Doc' Dowden helped the Dons to a 3-1 victory over Isthmian League champions Nunhead in a London Senior Cup first-round second replay played in front of more than 7,000 fans at Plough Lane. It was to be a year of triumph for the Dons as their all-conquering first team went on to win the Isthmian League and the London Senior Cup for the first time.

21st February 2009

Seeming to hit a divot before bouncing up over the despairing dive of Joe Woolley in the Thurrock goal, Sam Hatton's 84th-minute free kick gave the Dons their seventh successive Conference South victory. 'If winning a league is about winning ugly and getting breaks, then today we have achieved both,' manager Terry Brown said. 'It may turn out to be a massive three points for us, as results went our way. Chelmsford losing at Bognor was a real bonus.'

22nd February 1987

The Dons knocked holders Everton out of the FA Cup in a fifth-round tie that was screened live to the nation on the BBC. A goal behind to the league leaders early on, the hosts were level by the break before second-half strikes from John Fashanu and Andy Sayer took the Dons into the quarter-finals for the first time. 'Fashanu was immense,' admitted his marker, the Wales captain Kevin Ratcliffe. 'They pumped it to him in the air and he really got stuck in.'

22nd February 2003

An impressive Withdean 2000 outfit were left just nine points behind the desperately disappointed Dons with an incredible nine games in hand after winning 2-0 at Kingsmeadow. 'We are not good enough to win Combined Counties League this year and a lot of that is down to me,' manager Terry Eames commented. 'I am the one who has brought the players in, and I pick the team. The truth is we have not won any of our games against the top sides.'

23rd February 1991

Playing with pace and power, the Dons put five goals past an expensively assembled Tottenham Hotspur side at Plough Lane. 'We caved in at the end,' Spurs boss Terry Venables admitted. 'We got the score back to 2-1 and then Gary Lineker has a chance to make it 2-2 but their guy got a foot in. Then we collapsed. For a lot of the game the boys looked good, but at the end we were well-beaten.'

23rd February 1997

A well-taken goal from Vinnie Jones midway through the first half led to a 1-0 win at Arsenal and left the Dons 12 points behind Premier League leaders Manchester United with three games in hand. 'It was a great finish,' said Kinnear of the goal. 'Vinnie is having his best season for us. He does that sort of thing day after day in training but sometimes his disciplinary record overshadows his ability. We now face six games in 18 days that will make or break our season.'

24th February 1985

Several Crystal Palace fans threw their season tickets at chairman Ron Noades in disgust after the Dons had won a Second Division fixture at Selhurst Park 5-0. The so-called 'Team of the Eighties' looked extremely ordinary as a Paul Fishenden hat-trick and two more from Stewart Evans saw Dave Bassett's boys romp home in their first league visit to SE25. 'Wimbledon were brilliant today,' Eagles boss Steve Coppell admitted.

24th February 2001

Embarrassingly knocked out of the FA Cup by lower-league Wycombe in midweek, the Dons responded by putting five past QPR. 'We had a team meeting after the Wycombe game and agreed that we had let ourselves down,' two-goal Mark Williams revealed. 'I was devastated and did not sleep for two days. Lots of people were looking to see how we would bounce back, and we've done it. We have four games in hand and if we win them, we will be in the play-off zone.'

25th February 1976

A Southern League game that Yeovil Town boss Stan Harland described as 'a virtual title decider' saw the Dons gain a vital 2-1 win at Huish Park. Sadly, few in the 2,912 crowd witnessed much of the action due to thick fog in the Somerset area as Wimbledon responded brilliantly to John Clancey's early opener to come from behind with goals from Ian Cooke and Jeff Bryant. Allen Batsford's men were now in pole position for a Southern League championship and cup double.

25th February 1995

Two excellent goals from Efan Ekoku and a backs-to-the-wall defensive display were enough for the Dons to beat Tottenham Hotspur 2-1 in a Premier League match at White Hart Lane. 'That was a victory for the little men,' manager Joe Kinnear claimed. 'My defence cost all of £400,000 against an attack, including Jurgen Klinsmann, that was worth £12–15m.'

26th February 1951

A Monday afternoon Plough Lane crowd of nearly 10,000 fans saw the Dons finally dispose of neighbours Tooting & Mitcham United in the third replay of a long-running FA Amateur Cup third-round tie. Bob Parker had fired the Terrors in front with just two minutes on the clock, but the Dons fought back and two goals in five minutes early in the second half put the hosts in control before a third from Jimmy Smith, with just moments remaining, settled the contest.

26th February 2000

Twice ahead through Jason Euell and Carl Cort, the Dons were unable to hold on for an unlikely victory as Premier League leaders Manchester United scrambled a late goal at Selhurst Park. 'We are not cynical enough,' manager Egil Olsen said after watching Ryan Giggs run the entire length of the pitch in the 80th minute to set up Andy Cole's equaliser. 'That was a stupid goal to concede from our point of view.'

27th February 1973

Rickards Lodge schoolgirl Lynda Inchcombe was chosen as the Wimbledon supporters' Football Queen on the day the Dons went down 3-1 in a Southern League match at Ramsgate Athletic. According to a distinctly non-PC report in the local paper, the 17-year-old was the answer to falling attendances. 'Every inch of her 35-24-35 frame advertises herself as the ideal fan,' it gushed, 'we would have thought the fans would be tearing down the turnstiles to join her.'

27th February 1999

The Dons' first Premier League goal for 382 minutes provided a lift as Joe Kinnear's side battled to secure a point in a 1-1 draw at Goodison Park. 'Wimbledon are a very tough side to play against,' Everton boss Walter Smith commented. 'They impose themselves on the play and don't give you any time on the ball. Dave Watson got caught out by the wind for their goal and it was an uphill struggle after that.'

28th February 1979

Four goals from Alan Cork helped the Dons to a remarkable 6-1 win at Torquay United that kept their Fourth Division promotion hopes alive. 'I thought our teamwork was superb,' manager Dario Gradi said after the home side had been booed off at Plainmoor. 'I was particularly pleased for Alan Cork. He has been through a bad patch recently, but he has worked hard to rediscover his form.'

28th February 1987

A hat-trick from Andy Sayer earned the Dons a 3-1 win over Newcastle United but it was off-the-field events at Plough Lane that took the headlines. Several hundred fans stayed behind after the final whistle to show their opposition to the possibility of the club merging with Crystal Palace. 'We are dealing with realities, not fairytales,' owner Sam Hammam said in the week that followed. 'I will not allow supporters who do not know the financial facts to kill the club with their emotions.'

29th February 1992

The Dons stretched their unbeaten record under new manager Joe Kinnear to five games with a hard-fought win at Oldham Athletic. 'It was just like the old days,' goalkeeper Hans Segers said after watching Paul McGee score the winner. 'We were confident we could defend anything they could throw at us and still come away with a win. We are determined to be part of the new Premier League next season.'

29th February 2020

Callum Reilly scored a stoppage-time winner as the Dons ended a seven-game winless run in League One with a 2-1 victory at Gillingham. 'It has been a difficult February, but now we have picked up some points and this was a big win for us,' manager Glyn Hodges said. 'I felt hard done by when they got the equaliser because we had defended great. The lads did brilliantly to come again to get the winner. I felt we deserved it.'

AFC WIMBLEDON
On This Day

MARCH

1st March 1947

Superior in every department, the Dons trounced neighbours Sutton United 4-0 in front of 4,800 fans at Gander Green Lane to stretch their winning run to nine games. Two goals in each half were enough for Wimbledon to move into round three of the London Senior Cup as they advanced on four fronts – Isthmian League, London, and Surrey Senior Cups and the big one, the FA Amateur Cup, where they faced a semi-final against northern giants Bishop Auckland.

1st March 1969

A 1-0 win in Bedford's Eyrie was enough to extend Wimbledon's unbeaten run to ten and send Les Henley's team clear at the top of the Southern League table for the first time. Eagles centre-half Brian Stevens did his best to keep hold of the Dons' in-form centre-forward Gerry O'Rourke but when the Scotsman threw himself full length at Tommy McCready's knock-down in the 26th minute there was nothing the young defender could do to stop him scoring.

2nd March 1935

A record crowd of 18,080 packed into Plough Lane to see Wimbledon beat HMS *Victory* 3-0 in the FA Amateur Cup. The naval outfit had caught the public's imagination after finally beating a strong Leytonstone side following four replays in the previous round, but they proved no match for the Dons who were two up at the break thanks to strikes from the prolific W.W. 'Doc' Dowden. Any hope of another giant-killing ended when Eric Turner scored the third and final goal in the 57th minute.

2nd March 2002

A lone Daniele Dichio goal was enough to give West Bromwich Albion victory at Selhurst Park and extend the Dons' dismal First Division home record. 'We would have to win nearly all our remaining games if we are going to get into the play-offs,' manager Terry Burton conceded before complaining about a group of home fans. 'Some idiots behind me kept going on about getting the ball forward,' he said. 'If they want to see that sort of football they should go to the public park.'

3rd March 1962

Supporters of Wimbledon and Enfield shared a special train north to support their favourites in the quarter-finals of the FA Amateur Cup at Crook and West Auckland, respectively. With two inches of snow covering much of the Millfield playing surface, the Dons slid out of the competition following goals from Crook's Arnold Coates and Don Sparks. The travelling fans amused themselves in the second half by lobbing frozen projectiles at the aptly named Ray Snowball in the Town goal.

3rd March 1999

Joe Kinnear was reported to be in a 'comfortable' condition after suffering a heart attack in advance of the Dons' midweek Premier League match at Sheffield Wednesday. Taken to the city's Northern General Hospital with chest pains before kick-off, the manager missed seeing goals from Efan Ekoku and Marcus Gayle to give the visitors a 2-1 victory. It proved to be the end of an era as the 52-year-old never returned to his duties as Wimbledon manager.

4th March 1981

A late header from Alan Cork earned the Dons a point at Fourth Division promotion rivals Peterborough United. With three wins and three draws since taking over from Dario Gradi in late January, new boss Dave Bassett was cautiously optimistic about his team's chances. 'We're having to come from behind so draws are not really good enough,' the 37-year-old said. 'But Peterborough are up there so I have got to be pleased with the way we came back to steal a point.'

4th March 1989

Twenty-one-year-old striker Paul Miller fired a hat-trick past England goalkeeper Peter Shilton as the Dons continued their upward march by beating Derby County 4-0 at home. Despite having conceded just six goals in their previous ten away games, the Rams' defence was no match for the rampant hosts. 'At the moment we're flying so high we don't ever think we are going to come down,' defender Keith Curle said as Wimbledon moved into the First Division's top ten.

5th March 1952

Despite the game kicking off at 2.45pm on a Wednesday, 13,715 fans dodged work to converge on Arsenal's Highbury stadium to see the Dons fritter away the chance to progress into the quarter-finals of the FA Amateur Cup. After two drawn games had failed to separate the sides, the powerful Walthamstow Avenue team took a first-half lead and when Essex and England cricketer Trevor Bailey coolly lobbed Alan Hooper for the second goal the game was over as a contest.

5th March 2005

A lone Leon McDowall goal was enough to beat Molesey and take the Dons closer to promotion from the Ryman League Division One. 'We are 14 points clear at the top as we go into the run-in and now, we need to hold our nerve,' manager Dave Anderson said. 'I have to be careful with any predictions as there is still a long way to go but I guess four wins and two draws from our nine remaining games should be enough.'

6th March 1965

Two private planes took the Dons down to south Wales to face bottom-of-the-table Barry Town as a second-half hat-trick from Eddie Reynolds secured another Southern League First Division victory. Backed by two coaches of fans who swelled the Jenner Park gate to a season's record 542, Wimbledon were too often bogged down on the muddy surface and only improved after a half-time tongue-lashing from manager Les Henley.

6th March 2002

Seemingly happier away from the poisonous atmosphere at Selhurst Park, Neal Ardley's deflected goal gave the Dons yet another First Division away win, this time at relegation-threatened Sheffield Wednesday. 'Sheffield were really up for this game and started well but I was delighted by the way in which we responded,' manager Terry Burton commented. 'The winning goal was a bit fortunate, but we have deserved one of those for quite a while.'

7th March 1961

The gates were locked on a record Richmond Road midweek crowd of 9,870 before the Dons hit Whitley Bay for six in an FA Amateur Cup third-round tie. The second replay at neutral Kingstonian attracted huge local interest as Geoff Hamm masterminded the demolition of the plucky north-easterners. Brian Martin grabbed a hat-trick as Wimbledon won 6-1 to set up a quarter-final meeting with Walthamstow Avenue at Plough Lane.

7th March 2020

Kwesi Appiah had a headed goal disallowed as what proved to be the Dons' final match at Kingsmeadow ended in a 0-0 draw after a dour contest with fellow strugglers Bolton Wanderers. It turned out that fans were watching the final knockings of the 2019/20 campaign as the Covid-19 virus was soon to see the season suspended with Wimbledon relieved to find themselves just above the relegation zone.

8th March 1975

Despite dominating Scarborough for much of an FA Trophy quarter-final at Seamer Road, the Dons returned from north Yorkshire a beaten side. The visitors had hit the woodwork four times before Billy Edwards's weak back pass allowed the hosts to score a second-half winner. 'You must be joking,' manager Allen Batsford said when asked if he thought Scarborough would go on to win the trophy. 'They're not a good side. They would only finish in the bottom half of the Southern League.'

8th March 1986

Headed second-half goals from Alan Cork and Stewart Evans saw fourth-placed Wimbledon beat Second Division table-toppers Norwich City in SW19. 'Everyone says Norwich and Portsmouth are certs to go up – that's rubbish!' the Canaries captain said. 'Pompey's recent results have been dreadful. If I had to stick my neck out, I would say that Norwich, Charlton and Wimbledon will go up. Wimbledon are really difficult to play against and I have a great respect for them.'

9th March 1974

Relegation from the Southern League Premier Division looked a real possibility after the injury-hit Dons lost at home to bottom-of-the-table Hillingdon Borough in front of just 550 spectators. Beleaguered boss Dick Graham hit out at the club's board, saying, 'We need not have played that game. It was rearranged from an earlier date without my knowledge. When you consider how many key players we had missing, we were lucky only to lose 3-0.'

9th March 1996

A Dean Holdsworth header seven minutes from time earned Wimbledon the FA Cup quarter-final replay against Chelsea their stirring display deserved. Having taken the lead at Stamford Bridge, the visitors then found themselves behind before the substitute struck. 'When everyone thought that we were dead and buried we came back again,' manager Joe Kinnear said. 'It will be some replay I can assure you of that.' In the event, it was to be the Blues who eventually prevailed.

10th March 2012

Kieran Djilali scored the winner four minutes from time as the Dons beat rock-bottom Dagenham & Redbridge 2-1 in a tense encounter at Kingsmeadow. 'Today's game was "must-win" and now Tuesday's game against Bradford becomes "must-not-lose",' manager Terry Brown said. 'If you lose to Hereford, Plymouth, Dagenham and Bradford do you really expect to keep your job? I knew we had to win today, and we have found a way to do it.'

10th March 2018

Oxford's on-loan defender Todd Kane called for referee Christopher Sarginson to be sacked after he had conceded a penalty in his side's 2-1 defeat at Kingsmeadow. 'He just fell over me and the referee pointed to the spot,' Kane claimed. 'It's absolutely diabolical. Not even just the decision, the whole game – he needs to get fired from being a referee if I'm honest. You can't do anything about it.' The U's man was frustrated after seeing his side lose to Jon Meades's second-half goal.

11th March 1997

Simon Grayson's second-half header sent the Dons out of the League Cup, but it took a heroic performance from Kasey Keller and his Leicester defenders to see his team through to a Wembley final on the away goals rule. Marcus Gayle's drive from an acute angle had put the hosts ahead and the Foxes' goal led a charmed life during extra time. 'We played for 120 minutes,' visiting boss Martin O'Neill said. 'But it felt like 120 years in Alcatraz.'

11th March 2000

The Dons gained what proved to be their last Premier League victory by beating Leicester City 2-1 at Selhurst Park. 'The win was very important, not just for the points but for morale,' said coach Lars Tjærnås as the team moved six points clear of the relegation places. 'The players showed a real desire to win. [Carl] Cort and [Jason] Euell have asked to be put on the transfer list, but I feel they have a bright future here and we could do some great things. I hope that the players decide to stay.'

12th March 1994

New Manchester City chairman Francis Lee reacted angrily after seeing his side pushed deeper into the relegation mire following the Dons' 1-0 victory at Maine Road. 'I'd rather go down than play like Wimbledon,' he said. 'It keeps them in the Premiership, and it keeps them going but if we played like that our supporters would walk out.' At the end of the campaign, City just escaped the drop while Joe Kinnear's men finished sixth.

12th March 2013

The Dons came from a goal down to win 3-1 at Southend United and keep their League Two survival hopes alive. 'We didn't just beat them tonight – we made them look ordinary,' a delighted Neal Ardley said after goals from Pim Balkestein, Jack Midson and Luke Moore. 'We played with an attacking formation, and it paid dividends. With our win on Saturday and tonight, we are off the bottom, and we have given ourselves a fighting chance.'

13th March 2004

Unaffected by the suspension of manager Terry Eames the previous month, second-half goals from Joe Sheerin and Matt Everard helped secure a 4-1 win at Godalming and Guildford – the Dons' 31st Combined Counties League victory of the campaign. 'I am very confident in my ability to do the job,' caretaker boss Nicky English said as the club advertised for a new manager. 'Half the battle is knowing players and I have the contacts to bring top performers to this club.'

13th March 2021

Goalkeeper Nik Tzanev was the Dons' hero as a goalless draw with fellow League One strugglers Bristol Rovers gave Mark Robinson his sixth point in the seven games since he had taken over as first-team coach. 'Not picking up the wins is frustrating, but if people can't see the difference, I am wasting my time!' Robbo said. 'There is a difference with the work rate, the endeavour, and the fact we can keep the ball. Wins will come but we have to be patient.'

14th March 1967

The Dons' hopes of landing a Southern League championship and cup double were ended as they were well-beaten in a League Cup semi-final played in front of more than 4,000 fans at Barnet. Accompanied to north London by five coaches of supporters, Wimbledon never recovered after the prolific Les Easom gave the hosts a two-goal lead by the half-hour mark and eventually lost 3-1. Then, three defeats over the Easter weekend saw any hope of winning the league slip away.

14th March 1998

Manager Joe Kinnear greeted a narrow 2-1 victory over Leicester City with a clenched fist and went on to tell the media that his team needed just five points from their remaining ten games to ensure Premier League survival. Andy Roberts and Robbie Savage had exchanged goals before Michael Hughes hit the winner in the 62nd minute. One win and five goalless draws in those matches eventually saw the Dons limp over the safety line.

15th March 2008

Fortunate to be 2-1 up with 12 minutes to go, the Dons conceded two late goals to Chelmsford City, leaving them 13 points clear at the head of the Ryman League table. 'I realise that we are still mathematically capable of catching them but realistically we must now concentrate on cementing second place,' manager Terry Brown said. 'The sooner we can make sure we are runners-up, the sooner we can plan a strategy for the play-offs.'

15th March 2017

Making their inaugural visit to Kingsmeadow, Milton Keynes were well-beaten on a night when the sheer intensity of the crowd played a significant part in the Dons' victory. After a tense first half, Jake Reeves struck just after the hour before Lyle Taylor added a quick-fire second to record AFC Wimbledon's first league victory over their so-called-rivals. 'It means a lot more than three points,' Neal Ardley said afterwards.

16th March 2013

A superb chip from Jack Midson gave the Dons victory over fellow League Two strugglers Aldershot Town. 'It was sublime finish. Jack put in the effort for the team on a day when the forwards were surviving on scraps,' manager Neal Ardley said. 'We need to get to 50 points. Not all the teams down at the bottom will keep on winning and so that should be enough. We now have three wins on the bounce, and we have to keep our momentum going.'

16th March 2019

A lone Joe Pigott goal at Southend saw the Dons secure their third win in a row and move off the foot of the League One table. 'We were excellent at both ends today,' manager Wally Downes said. 'Joe held the ball up well and took his goal superbly and our back line secured their fourth clean sheet in a row. We have got a bit of a run going and now it is up to us to keep working hard. There is still time for us to escape the drop.'

17th March 1956

Angry spectators mobbed the referee at the end of an Isthmian League game against Leytonstone that had been marred throughout by deliberate fouls, arguments between players and the heckling of the crowd. Outplayed and outmanoeuvred, the visitors scored against the run of play with quarter of an hour to go and after the hapless referee had sent Joe Wallis off, he had to be escorted from the ground for his own safety.

17th March 1981

Tasting defeat for the first time in his eighth game in charge, Dave Bassett challenged his side to respond positively after they lost 4-1 at Darlington in controversial circumstances. Both Tommy Cunningham and Steve Galliers were sent off for dissent after disputing the Quakers' third goal, but the manager was still looking for his side to be promoted from the Fourth Division. 'The players have done so well to get us where we are and now, we will see whether they can handle the pressure,' he said.

18th March 1972

Andy Larkin was the hero as the Dons ended a run of nine successive Southern League away league defeats by winning at Merthyr Tydfil. Promoted from the reserve side, the 21-year-old amateur grabbed both goals in a much-needed 2-0 victory. 'I was finished after 60 minutes – really burnt out,' he said. 'But I was delighted to get the goals, really chuffed.' The game was a reward for the 50 or so loyal supporters who had followed the team to south Wales.

18th March 1995

Goals from Vinnie Jones and Marcus Gayle gave the tenant Dons a surprisingly easy Selhurst Park victory over their landlords, Crystal Palace. With the Dons up into the Premier League's top eight and the Eagles joining Chelsea and Manchester City in the relegation mire, Palace boss Alan Smith was furious. 'How eight of them can look me in the face and pick up their wages is beyond me,' he commented afterwards.

Joe Sheerin led the line and scored a brace as AFC Wimbledon steadied the ship after the suspension of manager Terry Eames.

19th March 1980

In front of the lowest crowd at the Manor Ground since Oxford joined the Football League in 1962, the Dons went down to a 4-1 defeat that all but confirmed their stay in the Third Division would last just one season. 'On that performance, Fourth Division football is about all we deserve,' disappointed manager Dario Gradi admitted. 'At one stage we had come right back into it only to throw it all away. This was meant to be the turning point.'

19th March 2016

The Dons' hopes of a League Two play-off place were kept alive by Jake Reeves's last-gasp wonder goal that defeated York City and secured a first win in six games. The game looked to be heading for a draw only for the midfielder to hit a perfect dipping volley in the third minute of added time. 'You need those moments,' manager Neal Ardley said. 'Let's hope it is a moment we look back on that changed the course of the season.'

20th March 1993

Skewering reputations throughout the first year of the Premier League, the Dons produced an excellent display to throttle the life out of title-chasing Norwich City at Selhurst Park. More than 10,000 fans saw the impressive Dean Holdsworth strike twice as Wimbledon stuffed the Canaries 3-1. 'I've scored 12 goals now, which was Joe Kinnear's target for me when I joined the club,' Holdsworth said. 'But that's not the end of it. There's plenty more goals to come.'

20th March 1996

The Dons were left licking their wounds after two late Chelsea goals saw them knocked out of the FA Cup at the quarter-final stage. Having played brilliantly when drawing the first match at Stamford Bridge, the replay was hanging in the balance at 1-1 before the Blues struck in the final ten minutes. 'I am bitterly disappointed,' manager Joe Kinnear reflected at the end. 'We matched them, and I thought this was the year we would reach Wembley.'

21st March 2006

The Dons crept back into the Ryman League Premier Division play-off positions for the first time since October as they made it three wins in four at Harrow Borough. Goals from Shane Smeltz and Wes Daly put Wimbledon in control but Boro pulled one back making the last few minutes nervous ones for the travelling fans. 'I feel I have the best squad since I came here,' manager Dave Anderson said. 'We are one of eight sides in contention for the play-offs and I feel the new lads will help us get there.'

21st March 2016

Ben Chorley's own goal was enough for the Dons to record a 1-0 victory against Portsmouth and leapfrog them in the League Two table. 'It doesn't matter how you win, you just need to win,' manager Neal Ardley said. 'It's been a tough three weeks, with the injuries to James Shea, David Connolly's retirement, Dave Winfield gets called back [to York City], Callum Kennedy and George Francomb get injured. And I fancied us to win despite all that. It's typical Wimbledon style, when going gets tough, we respond.'

22nd March 1947

Nearly 20,000 fans packed into Champion Hill to see the Dons beat Bishop Auckland 4-2 and advance to the final of the FA Amateur Cup. Former prisoner of war Ron Head inspired a brilliant two-goal burst in the opening ten minutes before the seven-time winners hit back and Wimbledon had to rely on a double from the evergreen Harry Stannard to see them through. The Dons were to face fellow Isthmian Leaguers Leytonstone in the Highbury final the following month.

22nd March 2014

Jack Midson's winner deep in stoppage time sealed a remarkable come-from-behind 4-3 League Two win for the Dons against Cheltenham. 'We learned soon afterwards that we were facing a points deduction [for fielding an ineligible player] and we decided not to tell the players,' assistant manager Neil Cox said. 'We were not looking at the play-offs anymore yet we had to stay focused. As a management team, our mindset had to change towards us staying up and that was hard.'

23rd March 1963

A brilliant, battling performance on Barnet's bone-hard Underhill pitch saw the Dons advance into the FA Amateur Cup quarter-finals. Unbeaten at home all season, the Athenian League Bees made Wimbledon work hard for the victory as they attacked down the slope after the break following Les Brown's first-half opener. But the best chance of the second period came when George Coote missed a late penalty for Wimbledon after Les Picking had handled in the box.

23rd March 1996

Trailing 2-1 after an hour at Goodison Park, the Dons stormed back through goals from Stewart Castledine, Andy Clarke and Jon Goodman to win 4-2 and ease their Premier League relegation worries. 'The dressing room is on fire,' manager Joe Kinnear said at the end. 'You just don't know what a big result this is for us and what a great psychological boost we will have for the final run-in. To take the points from a big club like this has done us the power of good.'

24th March 1984

With the *Match of the Day* cameras at Plough Lane to capture the action, the Dons overcame Walsall to win a crucial Third Division promotion battle. A characteristic header from Alan Cork gave the hosts the lead in the first half and when Wally Downes's cross-cum-shot went in off the far upright the points were secure. 'I aimed to hit it as near the goal as possible,' the midfielder claimed. 'They have to go in sometimes.'

24th March 2012

Record-signing Byron Harrison finally grabbed his first Dons goal as Wimbledon ended any lingering relegation worries by smashing managerless Burton Albion 4-0 at Kingsmeadow. 'The clean sheet said it all,' manager Terry Brown commented. 'It's our first one at home in the league – and that probably tells you a little bit about our season. I thought 4-0 flattered us in the end. Credit to Burton, I thought they came and attacked us for the whole game.'

25th March 2006

Paul Barnes was the star of the show as the Dons beat Wealdstone to move closer to securing a Ryman Premier League play-off spot. The centre-forward scored a perfect hat-trick, one with either foot and another with his head. 'You cannot have too many complaints after winning 5-1 away from home,' manager Dave Anderson commented. 'I thought we looked really impressive today with Paul Barnes proving a real handful up front.'

25th March 2016

Mayor of London Boris Johnson shocked AFC Wimbledon fans by deciding to 'call in' the plans for a new stadium on Plough Lane. Club chief executive Erik Samuelson said, 'I'm very disappointed. It's a decision to review the plans; it's not a decision to say no. We will represent our case strongly and clearly, and I still think it's an overwhelmingly positive case. We are planning and expecting that this is a delay and not a problem.'

26th March 1977

A defeat for long-time leaders Kettering Town meant the Dons moved to the top of the Southern League table for the first time after beating Maidstone United 2-1 at Plough Lane. With chairman Ron Noades away canvassing Football League club chairmen for votes as part of the 'Dons 4 Div 4' campaign, two goals from Ricky Marlowe took the team another step on the road to their third successive title.

26th March 2000

A wonder goal from West Ham's Paolo Di Canio led to a 2-1 defeat at Upton Park as the Dons' slide towards the Premier League trapdoor continued. 'We were poor, we deserved to lose and were lucky to only lose 2-1,' beleaguered boss Egil Olsen said. Michael Hughes scored the Wimbledon goal with a 30-yard drive, but his manager accused the midfielder of making 'big mistakes' in defence and being responsible for the Hammers' first goal.

27th March 1976

Teenage striker John Leslie scored four times as the title-chasing Dons won a Southern League match at Stourbridge 6-0. 'After scoring four, I thought that was it,' Leslie recalled. 'But [Allen] Batsford had a funny way of running things. He used to drop me to stop my head getting too big. And that is what happened after Stourbridge. They drew 1-1 against Atherstone without me, and Allen got a lot of stick in the paper for that decision.'

27th March 2007

The day after their punishment for fielding an ineligible player had been reduced to three points on appeal, the Dons celebrated by putting five past Leyton. 'The whole club has been lifted because of the appeal result,' manager Dave Anderson beamed. 'Now we know where we stand. The real task is to get promotion; I am delighted that we scored five goals today and now we have a good chance of making the play-offs.'

28th March 1987

Wimbledon's first visit to Anfield produced a dramatic win after a late goal from substitute Alan Cork. The visitors' all-round excellence in a 2-1 victory at the home of the league champions drew praise from the Liverpool hierarchy. 'It was hard to pick out their star player because it was such a fine team effort,' Reds coach Ronnie Moran said after the entire Dons backroom team had been invited for a post-match drink in the club's famed boot room.

28th March 2009

Alan Inns was sent off after the first goal in the Dons' 2-1 defeat in a top-of-the-table Conference South clash at Eastleigh was punched into the net by midfielder Tom Jordan. 'I asked the linesman why he had not flagged the handball and he said, "It is not my decision to make,"' the centre-back commented. 'When the referee came over, I told him we had been cheated, and I was shown the red card. It was such a big decision in such a crucial game, and I let my frustration get the better of me.'

29th March 1986

A ferociously hard-fought top-of-the-table encounter at Fratton Park ended all square after the introduction of the Dons' £125,000 record-signing John Fashanu had unsettled the home defence in the second half. 'I don't want to be drawn into a slanging match because that would be silly,' the big striker said after the home players had accused him of intimidation. 'Maybe there is a campaign to blacken my name if that is possible.'

29th March 1994

A brilliant four-goal blast after the break saw the Dons dent high-flying Blackburn Rovers' hopes of landing the title in the Premier League's second year. 'In the second half we were first to every tackle, every loose ball and Blackburn just didn't get a look in,' midfielder Peter Fear commented. 'The way we played in this match; we can beat anyone. I should not think Liverpool or Manchester United would want to face us in this form.'

30th March 1959

Without a game on Easter Monday, four coaches of supporters accompanied the Dons to the seaside for a friendly match against Eastbourne. They were pleased to see their favourites record a 2-1 win over their Corinthian League opposition but delighted when they heard that Isthmian League title rivals Wycombe had lost at bottom-of-the-table Leytonstone. Chairman Sydney Black was so happy that he stopped the team bus at a pub on the way home and ordered drinks all round.

30th March 1962

Slick finishing saw the Dons put seven goals past Hayes and reach the final of the London Senior Cup under the Kingstonian floodlights. The Athenian Leaguers worked hard but got no joy from an imperious Wimbledon defence and at the other end Eddie Reynolds scored four. With runaway Athenian leaders Enfield expected to win the other semi-final, all the talk was of a showdown in the final to establish the capital's finest amateur side.

31st March 1964

After a 4-2 Isthmian League win over Hitchin Town had seen the Dons close the gap on leaders Hendon, the club revealed its plans to turn professional in the summer. 'At the moment, we feel that the amateur game is declining,' treasurer Stanley Jasper said. 'We have sent out invitations to our 250 members for a special meeting on 11 May where we will discuss a proposal to join the Southern League.'

31st March 2001

Kevin Cooper's injury-time equaliser kept the Dons' slim play-off hopes alive as they twice came from behind to draw 2-2 with the First Division promotion-chasing Bolton Wanderers. 'I am happy with a point from a game that I thought had slipped away from us,' manager Terry Burton said. 'It's now 12 games unbeaten and I just wish we had started the season better. But we've still got 30 points to play for and seven of our last ten games are at home. We will not be giving up.'

AFC WIMBLEDON
On This Day

APRIL

1st April 1986

Closing in on promotion to the top flight, John Fashanu made a scoring debut as the Dons drew 1-1 with Crystal Palace. 'They get criticism because they seem to just feed one high ball after another into the box, but people should look at the quality of those balls,' Palace's Scottish international goalkeeper George Wood commented. 'They make life very difficult for any goalkeeper and back four.'

1st April 2013

A 1-0 home defeat at the hands of fellow strugglers Barnet left the Dons fearing for their Football League lives. With four games left, Neal Ardley's men were just three points above the relegation zone having lost two games in a row. 'We have looked tired in recent games, and we need one more push to get us over the line,' coach Simon Bassey was quoted as saying.

2nd April 1992

Two goals from John Fashanu and another from Robbie Earle saw the Dons comfortably beat a weary-looking Nottingham Forest side that were playing their third match in five days. Just 3,542 fans were inside Selhurst Park to watch Wimbledon's fifth top-flight victory in 11 games since Joe Kinnear had taken charge following the sacking of the disastrous Peter Withe. 'I thought Cloughie [Forest boss Brian Clough] took the defeat in the right manner,' the manager said.

2nd April 2016

After an indifferent run of results in March, Lyle Taylor scored twice to keep the Dons' League Two play-off hopes alive as they beat high-flying Wycombe Wanderers 2-1 at Adams Park. 'We were by far the better team,' manager Neal Ardley said. 'If you look at the chances, they had a few goalmouth scrambles, but we had four or five gilt-edged chances. I thought we were excellent.'

3rd April 1993

Promised a full-sized bust of himself if he scored 20 Premier League goals by the end of the season, Dean Holdsworth hit the net twice as the Dons lost 6-2 at Oldham Athletic. 'He is a cocky son-of-a-gun,' club owner Sam Hammam said. 'He has scored 15 goals in the league, just one behind [Alan] Shearer and [Teddy] Sheringham. He has got six games left to hit the mark.'

3rd April 1999

The Dons held a Manchester United side closing in on a historic Premier League, FA Cup and Champions League treble to a 1-1 draw at Selhurst Park. Jason Euell gave Wimbledon a sixth-minute lead, but David Beckham equalised before half-time. With Mick Harford and David Kemp in charge of the side following Joe Kinnear's heart attack, the point edged the tenth-placed hosts closer to safety and the prospect of their 14th year of top-flight football.

4th April 1964

Just a week after losing to the long-term leaders at Claremont Road, the Dons gained their revenge in the return and moved to within two points of Hendon at the top of the Isthmian League. Behind early on, Wimbledon had a huge slice of luck when the Greens' left-winger Peter Slade was stretched off in the 25th minute. Against ten men, the hosts dominated as goals from Roy Law and Eddie Reynolds helped Les Henley's boys move closer to a third successive title.

4th April 2009

A 2-0 win over a supine Team Bath side was just what the doctor ordered after successive Conference South defeats to Welling and Eastleigh had left Hampton just three points behind the top-of-the-table Dons with a game in hand. 'I am sure the supporters suffered as much as I did today,' manager Terry Brown said. 'These are certainly nervous times for all three teams that possess title aspirations. Until the first goal goes in in any of our next four games the pressure obviously mounts up.'

5th April 2005

Antony Howard booked a place in Wimbledon folklore as he engineered the greatest cup shock in the new Dons' brief history. Conference South side Sutton were hot favourites to win a Surrey Senior Cup semi-final, but the centre-back not only scored the decisive goal early in the second half but then took over between the posts when Paul Smith was injured late on. He had to make a couple of saves, as the referee allowed an agonising ten minutes of injury time, before emerging as the hero.

5th April 2008

Robin Shroot's 90th-minute winner allowed the nervous Dons to beat Billericay Town 2-1 and secure a Ryman League play-off spot. 'Stuart [Cash] and I have considerable experience of taking part in play-off games and we know the sheer delight supporters felt when their team is victorious and the despair that is felt if your side lose,' manager Terry Brown said. Fans were to experience a full range of emotions in the games against AFC Hornchurch and Staines Town that followed.

6th April 1968

After observing a minute's silence following the death of the club's chairman Sydney Black, a Plough Lane crowd of 3,843 saw an eagerly anticipated top-of-the-table Southern League clash with Cambridge United end in a draw after future Chelsea star Ian Hutchinson levelled Eddie Bailham's strike. It was to be years before those who ran the club learned to live without their erstwhile benefactor's cash.

6th April 2019

Despite Joe Pigott's 14th goal of the season, there was disappointment as the Dons could not make it five wins in six games when they drew with Accrington Stanley. With 11 clubs separated by just five points, the League One relegation battle was set to go to the last day. 'Three points would've been great, but you've got to respect the point,' March manager of the month Wally Downes said.

7th April 2001

Former FC Copenhagen striker David Nielsen marked his debut by scoring the first goal in the Dons 3-1 First Division victory over high-flying Birmingham City. 'We worked hard and got our reward,' manager Terry Burton said after seeing his side move up into tenth place. 'We still have plenty of points to play for and we will be doing everything in our power to reach the play-offs.'

Fan favourite Robbie Earle helped himself to a goal as Wimbledon eased past Nottingham Forest as their impressive form continued under new boss Joe Kinnear.

7th April 2010

A 5-0 defeat at York City ended the Dons' outside hopes of securing a Blue Square Premier play-off spot. 'After losing to Stevenage on Monday and here tonight we can't hide from the fact that we could not physically cope at the back,' manager Terry Brown said. 'After two thumpings my job is to keep the players heads up and we may have to adapt a more negative formation for the Mansfield game as our present cavalier approach is leading to us conceding too many goals.'

8th April 1950

The club's annual Easter tour saw the Dons play two games in Cornwall. After a crowd of 3,500 had seen a Harry Bull hat-trick in a 5-0 win against Penzance on Good Friday, a smaller crowd gathered 24 hours later to watch a Mousehole side lose 4-0. The 30-strong Wimbledon party was based at the Mount's Bay hotel on the seafront.

8th April 2004

A hat-trick from Kevin Cooper helped the Dons register a comfortable 5-0 victory over Coney Hall to reach the final of the Combined Counties League Challenge Cup. In injury time, a home defender handled the ball and Simon Bassey stepped up to take the kick but blazed the ball over the bar. 'I'm not talking about that penalty,' he said afterwards. 'I normally dink them, but I decided not to. Next time I'll dink it.'

9th April 1988

Demonstrating the awesome self-belief that had carried them to the very top, the Dons came from behind to beat Luton and reach Wembley at the end of a pulsating FA Cup semi-final played at White Hart Lane. Patrick Collins of the *Mail on Sunday* could not resist a sneer when he wrote, 'There was something disturbing in the sight of Vinnie Jones and his chums recklessly charging across the pitch where once [Tommy] Harmer, [Danny] Blanchflower and John White played a game we could understand and cherish.'

9th April 2011

Producing some of their best football of the season during a very one-sided first half at the Abbey Stadium, the Blue Square Premier Dons eventually emerged with a 2-1 victory after a late Cambridge United fightback had produced one or two jitters. 'The win today almost clinched our play-off spot, barring a Rory McIlroy-style end to the season,' manager Terry Brown commented, referencing the Irishman's recent final-round collapse at the Masters. There were to be more jitters in the games against Fleetwood and Luton that followed.

10th April 2010

After making six changes to the side that had lost 5-0 to York City in midweek, manager Terry Brown must have been delighted when Danny Kedwell's early goal secured a hard-fought Blue Square Premier victory at Mansfield Town. The real hero was Seb Brown who saved two injury-time penalties as the Stags threw everything at their visitors following the 58th-minute dismissal of Derek Duncan for elbowing an opponent.

11th April 1998

A hard-fought victory at The Dell all but guaranteed Wimbledon would be playing their 13th season of top-flight football the following August. Having failed to score in each of their previous three matches, the visitors were handed a gift when Southampton goalkeeper Paul Jones miskicked to allow Carl Leaburn the simple job of walking the ball into the net. 'Sometimes getting results is more important than the quality of your performance,' manager Joe Kinnear commented.

12th April 2000

A disastrous night in SE25 ended with Egil Olsen's Dons facing the very real threat of dropping out of the Premier League after losing 2-0 to Sheffield Wednesday. Despite his side's run of five successive defeats, the manager tried to sound confident. 'We are six points ahead of Bradford, Wednesday and Watford but still need to win at least one more match,' he said. 'It could come at Bradford but that will be like a relegation final, and I want us to pick up points before that.'

12th April 2004

A 3-0 victory at Walton Casuals confirmed the Dons as Combined Counties League champions. 'This was as good as it gets and it was a fantastic day,' manager Nicky English said. 'It has been a team effort, but I would say that the Danny Oakins/Matt Everard partnership at the back has been the rock on which our success has been built. Seb [Favata] and Gavin [Bolger] have been immense in midfield and up front Kevin Cooper has broken every known goalscoring record.'

13th April 1963

Seeking revenge for a 2-1 defeat at the hands of Leytonstone in the FA Amateur Cup Final 15 years earlier, more than 9,000 fans inside Arsenal's Highbury saw Wimbledon beat the same opponents, on the same ground, by the same score in the semi-final of the same competition. Goals from Brian Martin and Norman Williams had put the Dons two up before Roger Day pulled one back to set up a nervy finale before the club's first Wembley appearance was confirmed.

13th April 2013

After three successive 1-0 defeats, two Luke Moore goals helped the Dons draw 2-2 with Exeter City and keep their survival hopes alive. 'If I said confidence was high, I would be lying,' midfielder Harry Pell revealed. 'This is what sorts out the men from the boys. We are still positive about survival despite the way recent games have gone. We now face games against Gillingham and Fleetwood that will decide our future.'

14th April 2001

Despite his side's play-off hopes appearing to be almost extinguished following a home First Division draw with Barnsley, Gareth Ainsworth was in bullish mood after his first goal for the club. 'We're still in with a shout because once more other results have gone our way,' the winger claimed. 'We will need to win all our six remaining games which will be hard, but the lads are convinced we can do it.'

14th April 2018

Manager Neal Ardley hailed referee Mark Heywood's decision to award a stoppage-time penalty in the Dons' crucial 3-2 win at Walsall as 'brave' while his opposite number Dean Keates described it as 'an absolute embarrassment'. What was not in dispute was that after going in at half-time 2-0 down, by completing a stunning second-half comeback the visitors had given themselves a relegation lifeline. 'Today the boys were brilliant, but the fans were immense,' Ardley said.

15th April 1980

The club announced that every player was available for transfer after a 3-1 home defeat at the hands of Oxford United confirmed that the Dons would be relegated after just one season in the Third Division. 'We've already sold Steve Parsons and Les Briley for a combined total of £80,000 and now the chairman wants me to find another £40,000,' manager Dario Gradi told a press conference. 'It doesn't mean I am going to sell everyone, but we need money in order to rebuild for next year.'

15th April 2006

Antony Howard's stoppage-time goal secured a 3-2 win over East Thurrock and left the stuttering Dons just two wins away from a Ryman League play-off place. 'That's a massive result for us,' manager Dave Anderson admitted. 'I honestly thought it was a draw. We'd gone two up and then committed suicide within a minute as they drew level. In the end we hung on there and got the result.'

16th April 1979

A brilliant display produced a five-goal win as the Dons beat Torquay United to take a giant step towards promotion in just their second season in the Fourth Division. Having beaten the hapless Gulls 6-1 a few months earlier at Plainmoor, the result produced the biggest ever home and away winning margin in the club's Football League history.

16th April 1994

A goal from John Fashanu, scored from close range after Peter Schmeichel had fumbled the ball, was enough for the Dons to beat Premier League leaders Manchester United in front of 28,553 fans at Selhurst Park. 'We analysed the situation when United beat us in the FA Cup,' Joe Kinnear explained. 'I felt the only way to beat them was to play five in midfield and let their centre-halves have the ball, because they wouldn't cause us as many problems as their full-backs and wide players.'

17th April 1971

The 16-year reign of Les Henley came to an end following a home Southern League victory over Gloucester City. With the long-serving manager controversially ousted in February and then asked to carry on until a replacement could be appointed, Ian Cooke's 17th goal of the season secured a 3-2 victory. Afterwards, one of the senior players who had joined his former boss for a quiet celebratory drink was quoted as saying, 'I think the club will regret the day they sacked Les.'

17th April 1982

A 0-0 draw at Newport County made relegation from the Third Division seem inevitable. 'Five of our last six league games have been away and we have gained just two draws and it looks unlikely we will escape the drop,' manager Dave Bassett said. 'However, we have several home games coming up and we will be fighting like mad to make up ground.'

18th April 1981

A single-goal win at AFC Bournemouth – the Dons' fourth 1-0 victory in five games – left Dave Bassett's side on the brink of promotion. With four matches left, three of them at home, Wimbledon needed two more victories to guarantee a spot in the Third Division the following year. 'I was disappointed with our second-half display but at this stage of the season results are more important than performances,' the manager commented. 'A couple more wins and we will be over the line.'

18th April 2009

A Jon Main header three minutes from time secured a draw at Hampton that all but guaranteed the Dons the Conference South title. With Wimbledon fans standing up to four deep around the Beveree, the football gods smiled on the visitors as two Beavers defenders were lying prone on the ground following a collision when the club's leading scorer nodded home. 'Barring a disaster of unheard of proportions, we should be having one heck of a party next Saturday evening,' manager Terry Brown commented.

19th April 1947

Making only their second appearance in an FA Amateur Cup Final, the Dons went down 2-1 to a powerful Leytonstone side in front of a crowd of 47,000 at Highbury. Ahead after Harry Stannard's 11th-minute strike, the south Londoners did not put away other chances before the Stones hit back to score twice in the minutes leading up to half-time. In the last quarter of the game, first Ron Head and then Frank Lemmer hit the bar as Wimbledon tried in vain to force extra time.

19th April 1977

Wimbledon manager Allen Batsford and England cricket captain Tony Greig appeared together in a photoshoot at Plough Lane designed to promote the club's 'Dons 4 Div 4' campaign to gain Football League status. 'We'll have to get into the league now,' Greig quipped as he became a Dons director. 'It's impossible to get Southern League scores when I am abroad on tour.'

20th April 1991

Neal Ardley made his debut as the Dons won 2-1 at Aston Villa, their third successive away victory as they moved towards a seventh-placed First Division finish. 'I thought Ardley had a great game – he certainly did not look like a 19-year-old,' manager Ray Harford commented. 'A few more like him and we won't have any worries about the future. We played as well as we have played all season.'

20th April 2013

Second-half goals from Jack Midson and Jon Meades secured a draw at Gillingham that meant the Dons' fight to avoid relegation would extend to the season's final day. Needing just a point to be confirmed as champions, the hosts were quickly ahead, and it looked all over for Wimbledon when Danny Kedwell deftly headed in a left-wing cross from Chris Whelpdale. But the late fightback left a relieved Neal Ardley to say, 'If we can play like that next week then we will be OK, and I still believe. I don't think York or Dagenham can overtake us if we win against Fleetwood.'

21st April 2002

What turned out to be the last match in Wimbledon FC's proud 113-year history ended with fans turning their back on the pitch in disgust. With the club's owners determined to relocate to Milton Keynes, Dons supporters had staged a season-long series of protests and by the time of a 1-0 home defeat by Barnsley an FA decision on whether the relocation should be allowed was just weeks away.

21st April 2003

The sight of an entire side of Colston Avenue occupied by a sea of yellow-and-blue-clad fans brought a lump to many throats as AFC Wimbledon moved towards the climax of their first season with a second successive 5-0 win. Taking over Carshalton Athletic's ground for the day, Merton rivals Raynes Park Vale were totally outclassed by a Wimbledon side that, despite heading for a total of more than 100 Combined Counties League points, looked destined to miss out on promotion.

22nd April 1987

Dave Bassett's post-match comments took the headlines as two goals from Glyn Hodges allowed the Dons to fight back from 2-0 down to draw 2-2 with Tottenham Hotspur. 'Claesen cheated,' the manager raged after Belgian international Nico went down in a heap in the second half. 'If someone lobs a ball at you, you don't go down as if you have been pole-axed. I would hate to be on Belgium's side in a fight. No wonder Germany roared straight through them in the war.'

22nd April 2006

Despite playing for the whole of the second half with ten men after the dismissal of Scott Curley, a 59th-minute strike from Richard Butler was enough to give the Dons victory at Hendon and ensure a Ryman League play-off spot. With barely enough fit men to put out a side, the visitors' back line held out for half an hour after the leading scorer had latched on to Paul Barnes's through ball to fire home. 'We're all delighted,' said manager Dave Anderson. 'At the start of the season that was our aim [to reach the play-offs] and we've achieved it.'

23rd April 1931

Almost 7,000 fans inside Champion Hill saw the Dons secure their first Isthmian League title, by defeating Dulwich Hamlet, the only side that could have beaten them to the crown. With the visitors forced to play for most of the match with just ten fit men after an early injury to Dave Evans, 'Doc' Dowden set up right-winger Charlie Christie for the crucial goal in the 46th minute. Hamlet winger Smith saw his shot come back off the bar as the hosts searched for an equaliser, but Wimbledon held on to record a famous victory.

23rd April 2019

The Dons gave their League One survival hopes a huge boost as Steve Seddon scored a stoppage-time equaliser to hold leaders Luton to a 2-2 draw at Kenilworth Road. 'We went toe to toe with them,' manager Wally Downes said. 'We rode our luck a little bit, but that's going to happen when you come to the champions-elect. We had players blocking the ball, we had goalkeepers saving it, and strikers working hard. If you keep going you get your just desserts.'

24th April 1965

Eddie Reynolds took his season's total to 57 with four more goals – his third hat-trick in consecutive matches – as Wimbledon ended their first season of professional football by beating Merthyr Tydfil 4-0 at Plough Lane. John Nash, chairman of the Southern League, presented Roy Law with the First Division runners-up trophy after the game and said, 'Today I come here to congratulate you on promotion to the Premier Division. There is no reason why you should not do as Oxford United have done and go on to reach the Football League.'

24th April 2001

Neal Ardley scored the third goal on the night the Dons' hopes of an immediate return to the Premier League were all but dashed by a home draw with Crewe Alexandra. 'We've had a decent run with only one defeat in 19 games, but this was a disappointing result,' manager Terry Burton said. 'It was frustrating being 2-0 and then 3-1 up before we conceded those goals. There are three games to go, and it is still mathematically possible. We will keep going until someone says it isn't.'

25th April 1959

Wycombe Wanderers' hopes of becoming Isthmian League champions vanished after they were thrashed 4-0 in SW19 to leave the title chase a two-horse race between the Dons and Dulwich Hamlet. Left-half and captain Jim Wright was the hero after he opened the scoring with a brilliant 40-yard drive that many observers described as the best goal seen at Plough Lane since the war.

25th April 1977

A season's best Plough Lane crowd of 4,100 witnessed goals from John Leslie and Jeff Bryant help the Dons win a virtual Southern League title decider with Kettering Town. A magnanimous Derek Dougan put his arm round his managerial opposite number Allen Batsford at the post-match press conference before telling him, 'Well done, Allen! I hope you get the Football League status you deserve.'

26th April 1986

A 3-1 victory over Hull City left the Dons just two wins away from promotion to the top flight. 'The First Division is every player's dream and even if I only play ten games there it will be something,' Alan Cork said. 'We knew that if we were still in the race at Christmas we were in with a chance. It is great for players like me, Wally Downes and Mark Morris who not so long ago were in the Fourth Division.'

26th April 2002

Terry Burton was sacked by Wimbledon after repeatedly clashing with Charles Koppel over transfer policy and the proposed move to Milton Keynes. Matters had come to a head when the manager had ignored instructions to omit defender Peter Hawkins from the team for the game against Barnsley as it would have earned him a £10,000 bonus for passing a specified number of appearances. With the club claiming to be losing £20,000 a day and out of play-off contention, the chairman was keen to cut costs.

27th April 1976

What should have been a night of celebration as the Dons were presented with the Southern League championship shield for the second successive year turned into an evening of shame as a record six men were dismissed in the Dons' 4-1 victory over Wealdstone. 'Some of the things both teams did on that pitch were bloody silly,' admitted manager Allen Batsford.

27th April 2013

The Dons secured the win they needed to secure their Football League status after beating Fleetwood Town 2-1 at Kingsmeadow thanks to a 72nd-minute penalty from Jack Midson. The victory, coupled with defeats for both Barnet and Dagenham, meant Wimbledon ended the season two points clear of the relegation places. 'It is a fantastic achievement as this was a hell of a job when I took it back in October,' a relieved Neal Ardley was quoted as saying.

28th April 1962

A defensive display, marshalled by the outstanding Roy Law, saw the Dons gain the point they needed at Walthamstow Avenue to guarantee the Isthmian League title. The goalless draw left Les Henley's men five points clear of second-placed Leytonstone and with each of the east Londoners' two games in hand worth a maximum of two points, Wimbledon were champions.

28th April 1981

John Leslie's two goals in the first ten minutes settled any nerves and set the Dons on the way to promotion to the Third Division. 'We are better equipped this time than we were when we went up before, in terms of experience and playing strength,' manager Dave Bassett said after a 4-1 victory over Rochdale. 'The players have been magnificent and have done all I asked of them.'

29th April 2005

A 3-0 win over Dorking confirmed the Dons would be promoted to the Ryman League Premier Division. 'I fully expected to be given a lukewarm reception when I came in at the start of the season,' Dave Anderson commented. 'New managers are normally appointed when things are going badly, but it was different here. Now I have got to make sure we kick on next year.'

29th April 2008

Two-goal Jon Main helped the Dons move into the Ryman League play-off final after AFC Hornchurch were beaten 3-1 at Kingsmeadow. 'The night of the play-off semi-final was pretty special,' the prolific striker recalled later. 'The crowd was electric, and I was absolutely buzzing. There are times when Wimbledon fans really transform a stadium, and that was one of those nights.'

30th April 1994

Dean Holdsworth scored with a close-range header as the Dons beat Tottenham Hotspur 2-1 to move up into sixth in the Premier League. With Spurs and Everton among the clubs facing relegation, Vinnie Jones said that the visitors' attitude had not been good enough. 'At a quarter to five next Saturday afternoon some big teams will need very large amounts of toilet paper,' he said.

30th April 2000

Two debatable decisions turned the match and ultimately the season as a 3-0 defeat at Bradford City left the Dons in the Premier League's bottom three for the first time. 'The penalty was disgraceful, and it killed us,' John Hartson said after being sent off for dissent. 'The second goal was blatant handball, and I couldn't control myself. Those decisions could cost us our Premiership status.'

AFC WIMBLEDON

On This Day

MAY

1st May 1975

With just a point needed for the Dons to secure their first Southern League title, the players of Telford United formed a guard of honour as their opponents took to the field before a 1-1 draw allowed Ian Cooke to be presented with the giant trophy on the pitch at the end of the game. 'The boys have done tremendously well given all the games and the injuries we have had,' manager Allen Batsford said.

1st May 2007

A 1-0 Ryman League play-off defeat at Bromley ended the Dons' season and Dave Anderson's spell as manager. 'I don't think the club should have let Dave go,' striker Steve Ferguson said. 'All we would have needed was three new players to refresh the squad and I am sure we would have won the league next season. The players wanted him to stay. It is our fault we did not go up.'

2nd May 1959

The Dons' 3-1 win at Dulwich Hamlet brought the Isthmian League title to Plough Lane for the first time in 23 years. With Wimbledon 2-0 up early in the second half after a double from young Alan Burton, future Don Les Brown pulled a goal back to cause jitters among the travelling fans in the 5,000 crowd before Eddie Reynolds wrapped up the game and the championship with his 37th goal of the season.

2nd May 2006

With several of their best players injured or suspended, the Dons missed out on the Ryman League play-off final after being beaten 2-1 by big-spending Fisher Athletic. 'I am deeply disappointed but, on the night, I cannot have any complaints about the result,' manager Dave Anderson said. 'My biggest regret is that I had so many players unavailable.'

3rd May 1986

The Dons completed an astonishing four-year journey from the Fourth Division to the top flight with a 1-0 win at Huddersfield Town. 'I struck it so sweetly it was always going in,' Lawrie Sanchez said of his 61st-minute goal. 'It's a pity that it should happen like this, with two of their players sent off, but at the end of the season that will be forgotten. All people will remember is that we have got promoted to the First Division.'

3rd May 2008

The Dons ended their Ryman League heartache by edging out Staines Town to win promotion to the Conference South. With ten minutes to go, it looked as though the Dons had fluffed their lines for the third year running but goals from Luis Cumbers and Mark DeBolla allowed Terry Brown's side to come from behind to win amid ecstatic scenes at Wheatsheaf Park.

4th May 1963

Four goals from the head of Eddie Reynolds were enough for the Dons to defeat Sutton United 4-2 and lift the FA Amateur Cup. With extra time looming and the score locked at 2-2, Geoff Hamm got free on the right and sent in a cross that the tall Irishman was able to power home, and right on time he climbed highest again to convert Ted Murphy's centre. The most coveted prize in amateur football was heading to Plough Lane at last.

4th May 1991

Wimbledon fans invaded the pitch at the end of the final first-team game at Plough Lane, a 3-0 defeat at the hands of Crystal Palace. Afterwards, Sam Hammam went on to the field to speak to supporters who feared for the future. 'Much as we love it here, we must move,' he said. 'It is the price of progress. We have signed a seven-year deal to share Selhurst Park.'

5th May 1984

The Dons' 2-1 win at Sheffield United put them on the brink of promotion to the Second Division for the first time in their history. One man who was especially delighted was goalscorer Stewart Evans as he had twice been rejected by Blades boss Ian Porterfield earlier in his career. 'I had been winding Stewart up all week and he certainly took the chance to prove some people up here wrong,' manager Dave Bassett said.

5th May 1987

A late goal from Dennis Wise ensured the Dons followed their win at Manchester United the previous Saturday by beating Chelsea 2-1 at Plough Lane. With one game to play, a team written off as relegation certainties were closing in on a sixth-placed top-flight finish. 'Dennis still thought he was playing at Old Trafford where he was our best player,' manager Dave Bassett said. 'Tonight, he was way off form, but I am pleased that we have completed our fourth double of the season.'

6th May 2000

An afternoon of almost unbearable tension ended with the Dons moving out of the Premier League relegation zone ahead of a last day trip to The Dell. With home fans singing 'Womble 'til I die!', Aston Villa established a 2-1 lead before a John Hartson equaliser secured a precious point. 'That point has put us in the driving seat, but we have still got it all to do at Southampton,' manager Terry Burton said.

6th May 2011

A brilliant display of disciplined, counter-attacking football ensured the Dons returned from the Fylde coast with a two-goal advantage to take into the second leg of the play-off semi-final with Fleetwood. 'If you had given me a draw on the way up, I would have taken it,' manager Terry Brown said. 'So, I am not going to lie and pretend that I am not delighted to have won so well. However, Fleetwood will come down on Wednesday with nothing to lose. We have to be wary.'

7th May 1983

The Dons clinched the Fourth Division title with a five-star display to beat Blackpool at Plough Lane. 'We had none of this last season when we could really have used it. When you are on a winning run you really do make your own luck,' ever-present goalkeeper Dave Beasant said after seeing two first-half shots come back off the post and into his arms.

7th May 1994

An Everton side facing relegation after 41 consecutive seasons in the top flight came from behind to beat the Dons and preserve their Premier League status. Despite the promptings of a fanatical crowd, Wimbledon were two up inside 20 minutes before a mixture of excellent shooting and dubious goalkeeping allowed the Toffees to emerge victorious. 'We could have won, and we should have won but we didn't. It was very emotional out there,' manager Joe Kinnear said at the end.

8th May 1982

John Leslie's disallowed strike proved the difference between relegation and staying up as the Dons could only draw 0-0 at home to Bristol City. 'We were not good enough,' manager Dave Bassett said. 'They will be in for extra training tomorrow as I was not satisfied.' In the event, Wimbledon went down to the Fourth Division on goal difference despite a late unbeaten run that had brought safety within touching distance.

8th May 1986

The Dons' players seemed to have their minds on their forthcoming holiday in Ibiza as they drew 1-1 at Bradford City in the season's final match. Having won promotion to the top flight with a win at Huddersfield the previous Saturday, their return to Yorkshire was a low-key affair and by taking only one of their numerous first-half chances, the Dons missed out on the three points that would have left them as runners-up in the final table.

9th May 1931

More than 10,000 fans at Selhurst Park saw the Dons beat Kingstonian 1-0 to land the London Senior Cup for the first time. Forced to play for more than a third of the game without Fred Gregory who had been rushed to hospital with a serious injury, Wimbledon won through a lone Mick O'Brien goal in the second half. Despite breaking one of his vertebrae in his neck, the club captain returned in time to play the last few minutes before going up to receive the trophy.

9th May 1993

Manchester United fans in a record league crowd of 30,115 repeatedly invaded the pitch as the Red Devils ended the first Premier League season as champions after a 2-1 win at Selhurst Park. 'They played exceptionally well and deserve their success,' Dons boss Joe Kinnear commented. 'Having won 1-0 at Old Trafford, I would love to have done the double over them, but it was not to be. They are the best side and deserved to win.'

10th May 1947

Forced to play 13 games in less than a month to complete their season after the backlog caused by reaching the FA Amateur Cup Final, the exhausted Dons lost 3-1 to Kingstonian in the London Senior Cup semi-final at Champion Hill. Although the Dons were deservedly ahead after half an hour, the Ks scored three times either side of the break to emerge victorious and ensure that Wimbledon's brilliant campaign ended without a trophy.

10th May 1983

A late goal from teenager Paul Fishenden at Halifax Town preserved the Dons' 21-match unbeaten run. Having already won the Fourth Division title, the visitors blew their chances of ending the season with 100 points with a draw at The Shay. 'The players thought it was beneath them as champions to have to go to Halifax on a Tuesday night in May,' said a furious Dave Bassett at the end. 'It was the worst I have seen in many a long day.'

11th May 1979

Dario Gradi's Dons came from behind to beat York City 2-1 and gain promotion to the Third Division for the first time in the club's history. Trailing to Gary Ford's first-half strike, Wimbledon looked nervous until John Leslie equalised in the 62nd minute. Then, with tension rising, the hosts sealed third spot when leading scorer Alan Cork fired home with five minutes left to play.

11th May 2011

On a night of pure celebration, the Dons moved into the final of the Conference play-offs after hitting Fleetwood for six. Already two up following an impressive performance in the first leg, Kaid Mohamed scored in the first attack and from then on it was only a matter of how many the Dons would add. 'We know how much it would mean to the fans if we could win in Manchester,' midfielder Steven Gregory said. 'We would love to be able to do it for them.'

12th May 1961

More than 4,000 fans at Champion Hill saw the depleted Dons draw 1-1 in the London Senior Cup Final with Wealdstone. A Mickey Moore goal appeared to have given Wimbledon victory, but the Stones equalised late in the second half and when extra time failed to produce another score the cup was shared. The capital's premier knockout competition for amateur sides was devalued by the absence of the four Dons stars who had been picked for England's tour of Europe.

12th May 1977

With the Dons having been confirmed as Southern League champions for the third successive year when title rivals Kettering had lost 5-1 at Yeovil the previous night, the Wealdstone players formed a guard of honour as Wimbledon took to the field at Lower Mead. A goalless draw was followed by the players being presented with the championship trophy and individual shields, but the evening was marred when local youths smashed the windows of one of the coaches that had taken supporters to west London.

13th May 1967

One of four clubs entering the final Saturday of the Southern League season still in with a chance of being crowned champions, the disappointing Dons lost 1-0 at already relegated Bath City. Romford's win at Worcester City took the title to east London as Billy Horton's long-range winner ruined Wimbledon's day. Three controversial decisions enraged the travelling fans at Twerton Park and the referee was jostled as he left the pitch at the end.

13th May 1995

For reasons that still remain unclear, an elephant was paraded on the pitch before the Dons' final game of the season, a 2-2 draw with Nottingham Forest. 'If any other Premiership team had been through half of what we have, they wouldn't have survived,' manager Joe Kinnear said after his team had secured a ninth-placed finish. 'We at Wimbledon are known for our total dedication and tremendous team spirit and we have needed both this season.'

14th May 1988

The Crazy Gang beat the Culture Club as the Dons' 1-0 win over First Division champions Liverpool brought the FA Cup back to the unlikely surroundings of Plough Lane. A first-half headed goal by Lawrie Sanchez and a penalty save from Dave Beasant after the break made it a day to remember for the Wimbledon fans in a Wembley crowd of 98,000 and a global TV audience estimated at more than 400 million.

14th May 2000

Spectacular second-half goals from Southampton's Wayne Bridge and Marians Pahars ended the Dons' 14-year stay in the top flight. Interim manager Terry Burton was almost lost for words at the end of the match. 'This has been a desperately disappointing day for our supporters, but it is our responsibility, me and the players, to start rebuilding and to bring this club back up,' he said.

15th May 1981

Sam Hammam assumed full control of Wimbledon Football Club. Ron Noades's takeover of Crystal Palace in January had left him in charge of two clubs, but the Lebanese businessman announced he had now bought enough shares for a controlling interest at Plough Lane. 'Running both clubs would be like having two wives and trying to love them equally,' he explained. 'I was best man at Ron's wedding but that has nothing to do with business or football.'

Captain Dave Beasant made history as the first goalkeeper to save an FA Cup Final penalty and help the Dons to an incredible victory against Liverpool.

16th May 1988

A crowd of 7,100 converged on Plough Lane as Alan Cork's testimonial match provided an excuse for the players to parade the FA Cup that they had won at Wembley just two days earlier. In response to chants from the crowd, the players bared their backsides to the West Bank, leading the FA to charge the club with bringing the game into disrepute. The nine players who dropped their shorts were eventually fined £750 per buttock while the club had to pay out £5,000.

17th May 1977

Wimbledon FC played their last game as a non-league club as they beat Staines Town 1-0 to win the London Senior Cup at Champion Hill. Despite the first-half dismissal of Dave Bassett, the ten-man Dons proved too strong for their Isthmian League opponents and won when teenager John Leslie scored the winner in the second period. Afterwards, manager Allen Batsford heaped praise on a defence that had conceded just eight goals in the final 21 games of the season.

18th May 2016

Lyle Taylor's extra-time strike sent the Dons through to the League Two play-off final after beating Accrington 3-2 on aggregate. Trailing 1-0 from the first leg, Stanley were leading 2-1 on aggregate by the hour only for Adebayo Akinfenwa's powerful header to level the scores. Jake Reeves's brilliant run and shot in the 104th minute allowed Taylor to hit home the rebound and take the Dons through to meet Plymouth at Wembley.

19th May 1976

Wimbledon beat Siracusa 3-0 in the first match of the post-season Anglo-Italian Cup – a competition for top non-league sides in England and Italy. Enraged that Ian Cooke's 27th-minute opener had been allowed to stand as they believed their goalkeeper had been fouled in the build-up, the Italian side spent the last hour moaning, diving and going in late as the game descended into farce. Police had to be called in as the fist-waving Sicilians were jeered from the pitch by incensed home fans at the end.

20th May 1969

An end-of-season testimonial game against Chelsea was wrecked as football hooliganism came to Plough Lane. Gates were broken down and one of the crossbars was snapped in half as visiting fans in the 5,250 crowd went on the rampage. 'I have never seen anything like it in 25 years of following football,' club chairman Len Hibberd commented in the aftermath. 'When they invaded the pitch, I thought that anything could happen. It was a miracle that no one was seriously hurt.'

21st May 1963

Continuing to clear the backlog of league fixtures caused by the winter freeze and their glorious FA Amateur Cup run, the Dons closed in on the Isthmian League title after a hard-fought 2-2 draw at Sandy Lane. The visitors were two up at half-time, but Tooting hit back after the break and when Gordon Holden equalised from a last-minute spot kick it was greeted with a deafening roar and a pitch invasion involving the black and white half of the 4,600 crowd.

21st May 2011

Seb Brown saved two Luton penalties to set Danny Kedwell up to shoot the Dons into the Football League. 'I took my daughter to the play-off final, and we were both nearly in tears when Danny Kedwell scored that penalty,' supporter Barry Faust recalled. 'I was happy for so many people. Not just the club or myself, but for Ivor Heller and the others who started it all. I was thinking about them with tears in my eyes, I wanted to thank them and all the players for making a dream come true.'

22nd May 2005

Dave Anderson was named Ryman League Division One manager of the year after guiding the Dons to the title in his first year in charge. 'I am very pleased and honoured,' he said. 'It has put the icing on the cake at the end of a fantastic season. I say this a lot, because it is true, but what we've achieved this season has truly been a team effort. So, I regard the award as a joint one, won by all the management team, not just me.'

23rd May 1989

Selected to face Chile at Wembley, John Fashanu became the first Wimbledon player to earn a full England cap. 'Don Howe and I had a love-hate relationship,' the tall striker recalled of the international team's coach. 'He hated me. He criticised me, the way I did things, the way I played, but I loved him. And then out of the blue he told me I was in the England squad. I couldn't believe it.'

23rd May 2004

An open-top bus carried the Dons' unbeaten Combined Counties League and cup double-winning squad through the streets of Wimbledon and to a civic reception at the town hall. 'Winning both the cup and league is a great achievement,' said Merton Council leader Andrew Judge. 'Not only is it an achievement for the club but it is a proud day for the people of Wimbledon. I hope they go on to achieve even greater things.'

24th May 1987

New manager Bobby Gould was quoted as saying that he was not bothered by the shortage of cash at Plough Lane on the day he was introduced to the press. 'I have left behind a tiny budget at Bristol Rovers and so I am used to it,' he said. 'Dave Bassett and Alan Gillett have left me a good squad to build on. I am delighted to have Don Howe with me. You only have to look at his record at Arsenal, where he produced so many good players, to see the quality of the man.'

25th May 1963

Eddie Reynolds's 53rd goal of the season ensured an FA Amateur Cup/Isthmian League double for the Dons at Green Pond Lane. Anything better than a seven-goal defeat at Walthamstow would have ensured the title and the exhausted Dons – playing their tenth game in May – won the game ten minutes from time when Mickey Moore crossed, and the tall Irishman headed the ball past goalkeeper Gary McGuire.

26th May 1960

The Dons announced that a £5,000 set of floodlights were being installed at Plough Lane meaning that matches could be played on winter evenings for the first time. 'I am confident that they will be the best in amateur football,' club chairman Sydney Black said. 'If need be, we can increase the pylons in both height and power.' Arsenal had agreed to switch their 'home' London Challenge Cup tie in October to Wimbledon to allow the new lights to be turned on officially.

27th May 1965

At a special dinner held at the Wimbledon Hill Hotel, the club received an illuminated address from the Football Association to mark the 75th anniversary of their birth in 1889. FA councillor D.W. Mackensie commented in his speech, 'Wimbledon have always strived to make progress. Having reached the top of the amateur game you decided to turn professional last summer. Many doubted the wisdom of this action. But having seen your performances and promotion in the Southern League we can see that the club is in good hands.'

27th May 2007

Terry Brown made his first signing when he brought Jason Goodliffe to the club. 'I said from the beginning that we didn't want to lose any of a back four that let in only 36 league goals last season,' the new manager said. 'The club had already secured Frankie Howard and Michael Haswell by taking up their contract options and now we've signed another quality player in Jason Goodliffe. He has played almost all his career in the Conference, and he is a natural leader.'

28th May 2002

A three-man FA Commission decided, by a two-to-one majority, to endorse the move of Wimbledon FC to Milton Keynes. The Wimbledon Independent Supporters Association (WISA) immediately vowed to continue the fight against the franchising of football and announced an open meeting to discuss the possibility of setting up a new club. 'I think it is a great idea,' said recently sacked Dons manager Terry Burton. 'If that is where the fans are, that is where the club will be.'

29th May 1962

Speaking at a dinner to celebrate winning the Isthmian League title, club president and Wimbledon MP Sir Cyril Black showed remarkable prescience when he told 200 guests, 'Few amateur clubs have such an impressive record and next season I am confident that they will win the Amateur Cup. Wimbledon are undoubtedly the premier amateur club in the country and their achievements bring credit and distinction to the whole town.'

30th May 2016

Lyle Taylor and Adebayo Akinfenwa fired the Dons to promotion in the League Two play-off final at Wembley. In a game that produced few chances, it took until the 78th minute for Taylor to make the breakthrough as he slotted the ball past Plymouth goalkeeper Luke McCormick. With several minutes of injury time already played, Wimbledon were awarded a penalty which Akinfenwa powered home.

31st May 2002

The founders of the newly formed AFC Wimbledon agreed a deal with Rajesh Khosla to play their home matches at Kingsmeadow. 'We were in a race against time,' Ivor Heller recalled later. 'We had just 12 days to get a groundshare deal signed, sealed and delivered. We had other offers, from clubs like Leatherhead and Dulwich, but I knew we needed to be close enough to our home community to call ourselves Wimbledon.'

AFC WIMBLEDON
On This Day

JUNE

1st June 1968

Len Hibberd sounded a note of caution about the club's finances after being announced as the new chairman in succession to the late Sydney Black. 'I have two years to cut costs by £7,000 per annum and the only way to do it is by using volunteers,' he was quoted as saying. 'When we had Mr Black around to write out a cheque each year, we were fine. But we have to pay our own way from now on.'

2nd June 1999

Joe Kinnear resigned as manager due to ill health, having been in charge since 1991. 'It was an immensely difficult decision to make,' the man who had suffered a heart attack before a match at Sheffield Wednesday the previous March said, 'but I felt I owed it to Sam [Hammam] and Wimbledon to be up-front about my decision rather than springing it on them only when I had sorted myself out.'

3rd June 1961

Chairman Sydney Black reported at the club's AGM that the average attendance for league matches at Plough Lane had increased to just below 3,000 in the 1960/61 season. But he went on to reveal that many of the team preferred playing away from home where they received less abuse from the terraces. 'Amateur footballers can't be expected to play brilliantly every week,' he said. 'If they did, they would not be playing for Wimbledon. Our players deserve more encouragement!'

4th June 1976

Despite being double Southern League champions, the Dons gained just three votes at the Football League's AGM in London as Stockport County, Newport County, Southport and Workington were all re-elected. 'A new approach is needed,' said clearly frustrated manager Allen Batsford as he reflected on the fact that a Yeovil side that had finished runners-up in league and cup secured 15 more votes than Wimbledon.

5th June 1959

At a town hall reception to celebrate the club's first Isthmian League title for 23 years, the mayor of Wimbledon, Alderman Clarke, congratulated the team on their success before raising expectations. 'Next season we hope you go one better and bring back that cup,' he said. The trophy he was referring to was the FA Amateur Cup – the Holy Grail as far as amateur teams like the Dons were concerned.

6th June 1975

Despite winning the Southern League and capturing the back-page headlines during their FA Cup matches with First Division sides Burnley and Leeds United, Wimbledon gained just four votes in the Football League's annual re-election ballot. Kettering Town, who had finished runners-up to the Dons, took 20 votes and came closest to toppling Workington – the sitting Fourth Division side with the least support.

7th June 1974

Allen Batsford, the 41-year-old former Arsenal player, was announced as the Dons' new manager. Despite the club being in dire financial straits and having just seven players on the books, the job was still attractive enough for 27 men to apply. 'Hendon came on strongly, but I thought long and hard about the decision,' the man who had achieved enormous success at Walton & Hersham said. 'I chose Wimbledon and now I am looking forward to the challenge.'

8th June 1976

West London businessman Ron Noades bought a controlling interest in Wimbledon FC. The new chairman's first act was to axe the club's old guard – 71-year-old former chairman Jack Beaven and his brother Fred – as a 13-man committee was installed. 'There can only be one target this season – Division Four,' the 39-year-old said. 'We have won the Southern League title twice in a row and it is going to be very difficult to make it a hat-trick.'

9th June 1964

The Dons ended 75 years as an amateur club when they were elected unopposed to the semi-professional Southern League after being nominated by former Isthmian League rivals Romford. 'We made the same move five seasons ago,' the Essex club's chairman M.J. Parrish said. 'It was the best thing we ever did, and Wimbledon will find the same. They have a wonderful ground, provide great hospitality, and have a chairman who intends to take them places.'

10th June 2021

Local MP Siobhain McDonagh described AFC Wimbledon in parliament as a shining example of how football should be run. 'Our club was stolen 60 miles up the M1 – an event that began one of English football's greatest stories,' she said. 'The Dons Trust now owns AFC Wimbledon, giving fans control of the future of our club and – after six promotions in 13 seasons – we soared our way to League One … it is a club that gives its heart and soul back to the community in which it belongs.'

11th June 1960

The Dons won 6-1 at Interlaken on a two-match post-season tour of Switzerland. Not allowed to pay players, chairman Sydney Black was able to attract and retain a squad of top amateurs by ensuring that they were, in the words of midfielder Bobby Ardrey, 'spoiled rotten'. In the age before overseas travel was the norm, such all-expenses-paid continental trips were part of what the club offered prospective players.

12th June 1958

Sydney Black met Geoff Hamm in a lay-by off the A3 to agree a deal to sign the England amateur international from Woking. In an age when the Isthmian League's motto was *Honor Sufficit* (Honour is Sufficient), paying players was strictly forbidden but having helped the Cards to an FA Amateur Cup triumph the midfield playmaker took Wimbledon's shilling and went on to play a crucial role as the Dons won their first league title for 23 years.

13th June 2002

A special meeting of the Dons Trust heard the news that AFC Wimbledon Ltd had been formed. During the same evening Terry Eames was introduced as the new club's first manager, the club crest and playing kit were unveiled and it was announced that more than £70,000 had been pledged to the new launch fund. With the new season approaching fast, player trials on Wimbledon Common were shortly to take place.

14th June 1998

Robbie Earle scored Jamaica's first goal in the World Cup finals, as the Reggae Boyz went down 3-1 against Croatia. 'I turned away as soon as I headed it. I knew it was in,' the long-time Wimbledon stalwart said later. 'We lost the game, but we were not disgraced. For all of us, it was overwhelming. This was the World Cup. It was an amazing atmosphere and none of us had ever played on a stage like that. In the end our inexperience told. We did not know how to control the excitement.'

15th June 1936

Five goals from young Harry Stannard helped Wimbledon beat Viborg 7-5 to win a summer tournament in Denmark. Travelling by sea and rail, a Dons side that had become well known when reaching the FA Amateur Cup Final a year earlier spent ten days on the continent, playing six matches and drawing large crowds wherever they went. The prolific Bill Charlton, who was shortly to transfer to QPR, surprisingly failed to get on to the scoresheet.

16th June 1976

The Dons lost 1-0 to Siracusa in the Anglo-Italian Cup. Despite having two men sent off and four booked, the nine-man Sicilians proved too strong as Wimbledon lost their first game of the tournament in 80-degree heat. Ian Cooke lost his cool and was booked for the second match running as the frustrated Dons chased the game late on but their earlier results in England proved enough for the side to reach the final against Monza.

17th June 1977

Three-time Southern League champions Wimbledon were elected to the Football League. Months of hard work and canvassing were rewarded when, at Football League's AGM at London's Cafe Royal, the results of the election ballot were announced as follows: Altrincham 12 votes, Halifax 44 votes, Hartlepool 43 votes, Southport 27 votes, Workington 21 votes, Wimbledon 27 votes. The Dons finished above Workington, taking their place in the Fourth Division.

18th June 2014

The Dons found out they would be able to submit a planning application for a new ground in Merton, near to where the old Wimbledon FC played. 'If you'd said to any of our fans on 28 May 2002, "Don't worry – 15 years from now you'll be in the Football League and opening a brand-new stadium in Plough Lane," they'd have said you're absolutely nutty,' chief executive Erik Samuelson said. 'It's a distance away, as I try to manage people's expectations, but it is within sight. What an achievement that would be, and what a story.'

19th June 1976

The Dons lost the Anglo-Italian Cup Final 1-0 to Monza in front of a highly partisan 4,487 crowd on the outskirts of Milan. Eight minutes after Roger Connell had been controversially sent off, Dickie Guy chested down a long ball on the edge of his box and was penalised for handball. The resulting free kick hit Ian Cooke and deflected into the path of Casagrane who fired home. 'We feel as though we have been kicked from one end of Italy to the other in these matches,' Batsford commented at the end.

20th June 1937

The Dons beat Ystads IF 3-1 during a four-match summer tour of Sweden and Denmark. Such trips involving top amateur clubs were common during the interwar years as the 'English' game of football spread across the continent. The match was played as the drumbeats of war sounded ever louder: the German Luftwaffe's recent bombing of the Spanish town of Guernica was one of many incidents that meant several of the young men involved that afternoon would shortly be swapping football kit for khaki.

It was Brazil or Wimbledon for Egil Olsen, and ultimately it was south-west London for the wellie-wearing Norwegian manager.

21st June 1985

In the wake of the fatal fire at Bradford, the Greater London Council inspectors decided that the wooden South Stand at Plough Lane was potentially too dangerous to be given a safety certificate. With capacities being reduced and exit routes being improved at sports stadia around the country, the Dons would begin their first season of Second Division football with only the North Stand available for fans to sit down.

22nd June 1986

FA secretary Ted Croker used a speech on the future of football at Keele University to outline a plan for a new 'super league' with no promotion and relegation – and his vision clearly did not include the Dons. 'It is delightful and romantic for Wimbledon to get from the Fourth Division to the very top, but their facilities are totally incapable of staging First Division football,' he said. 'To bring top clubs like Manchester United and Tottenham to a ground like that is ridiculous.'

23rd June 2002

Rejected by the Ryman League, the Dons were voted into the Combined Counties League instead. With the new club already having 450 season ticket holders and Kingsmeadow to use as a home ground, they were quickly installed as favourites to win the title in their first season in a league comprising mainly of teams from Surrey, Hampshire, Berkshire and west London.

24th June 1995

The Dons lost 4-0 to Bursaspor in the Intertoto Cup. Under pressure to participate after UEFA threatened to expel English teams from all European competitions if Premier League teams did not take part, a 'Wimbledon' side including several Manchester United youth players, a goalkeeper from Colchester United and Northampton Town's player-coach went down tamely in Turkey, the last of their four games in the tournament.

25th June 1970

With the Football League discussing the possibility of the formation of a fifth division in time for the 1971/72 campaign, a special meeting of the supporters' club was held at Plough Lane to hand over a cheque for £2,250 to the parent club. 'We need you to raise a very substantial amount more money this year,' chairman Stanley Jasper told fans. 'We are doing all we can to control costs but to achieve anything we must have your maximum support over the next year.'

26th June 1981

Six first-team players announced that they would not play for the club again unless they were given improved contracts before the start of the new season. Wally Downes, Gary Armstrong, Mick Smith, Tommy Cunningham, Paul Denny and Steve Jones were all in dispute, with captain Cunningham quoted as saying, 'We're only after what we deserve. We haven't had a rise for two years and after winning promotion last year we think we are due a bit more.'

27th June 1988

Dave Beasant signed for Newcastle United for £900,000 – a world-record fee for a goalkeeper. Having stunned football with his penalty save in the FA Cup Final at Wembley, club captain 'Lurch' moved north in search of a more lucrative contract. With chairman Sam Hammam having announced publicly that the entire squad was available for sale, there were expected to be further departures in the weeks that followed.

28th June 1992

The Dons made their first £1m signing when they captured Dean Holdsworth from Brentford. 'When I looked at Dean's record of around 70 goals in two seasons, I was impressed,' said manager Joe Kinnear. 'He oozes confidence. He doesn't just think he can score goals in the Premier League; he believes it with a passion. I think he will prove a great partner for John Fashanu.'

29th June 2002

Trials for places in AFC Wimbledon's first squad were held on Wimbledon Common. Manager Terry Eames was helped by ex-players Jeff Bryant, Lee Harwood and Steve Galliers as he whittled down the 230 hopefuls into a group suitable to take on the might of the Combined Counties League. The organisers had expected around 60 players to turn up and were overwhelmed by the enthusiasm that the new club was generating.

30th June 2014

AFC Wimbledon announced the signing of the experienced Adebayo Akinfenwa as preparations for the 2014/15 campaign began in earnest. 'If you put someone alongside him with the finishing prowess of Matt Tubbs then it is clear what I am trying to do here,' manager Neal Ardley was quoted as saying. 'I am over the moon to have got both of them.'

AFC WIMBLEDON
On This Day

JULY

1st July 1955

Sydney Black moved fast after taking over as the club's new chairman by sweeping away the old system of picking the team by committee and appointing Les Henley as the Dons' first full-time professional coach. 'I shall have full power of selection, so I am prepared to take any credit or brickbats,' the former Arsenal and Reading player revealed. 'I think if we work hard there is a reasonable chance of success.'

2nd July 1977

The players returned for pre-season training ahead of the Dons' first season in the Fourth Division with the club making headlines by announcing that they would be staying part-time. 'Most of the lads have good jobs and do not want to give them up,' goalkeeper Dickie Guy explained. 'I do well from my football and my job at the West India docks. How can I afford to go full-time at my age? We have always trained hard, and I see no reason why we cannot still be successful at a higher level.'

3rd July 2006

Multimillionaire businessman Darragh MacAnthony's bid to buy AFC Wimbledon was turned down by the club's board. With supporters reflecting in the wake of defeat at Fisher Athletic in the Ryman League play-offs, some believed a fresh cash injection was required. However, with memories of the battle to prevent Wimbledon FC moving to Milton Keynes still fresh, most favoured rejecting the Irishman's advances.

4th July 2007

Terry Brown set out the task ahead after supervising his first training session at AFC Wimbledon. 'I have been brought in to get the club out of the Ryman League,' the 56-year-old explained. 'We are pleased with the quality of player we have been able to bring in, but we are still looking to add to the squad. The starting fitness levels are good, but the players know that there is a long, hard road ahead if we want success.'

5th July 1971

New manager Mike Everitt was determined that his team would be among the fittest in the Southern League as he included weight training and five-mile runs across Wimbledon Common as part of the pre-season schedule. 'Everyone has worked really hard, and they seem to have enjoyed it,' he said as the first friendly approached. 'They are a lot stronger and fitter than when I saw them play at the end of last season.'

6th July 1975

As his Southern League title-winning side returned for pre-season training, manager Allen Batsford was cautiously optimistic about the campaign ahead. 'At the moment, the squad is looking very good,' he said, 'and I will be very disappointed if we are not there or thereabouts at the end of the season. Things will be harder for us this season as we got off to a flying start last year. This time clubs will be ready for us from the word go.'

7th July 2015

Better pedestrian access, more cycle facilities, and changes to the proposed East Stand of AFC Wimbledon's new stadium were announced after months of consultations with bodies including the Environment Agency and Wandsworth Council. Discussions with Merton Council's planning committee over the multimillion-pound bid for the club's homecoming to Plough Lane were set for later in the year to allow time for further public scrutiny of the plans.

8th July 2004

A Fans' Club, a brand-new play by Matthew Couper based on the true story of the formation of AFC Wimbledon, opened at the New Wimbledon Theatre. Telling the tale of the supporters' battles to save the club from moving to Milton Keynes and set up the new Dons, it featured one of Britain's leading actors in Alun Armstrong. 'We're the fans, we're back and we're doing what they said was impossible. Come and join the celebration,' the *New Tricks* star was quoted as saying.

9th July 2011

Just 49 days after Danny Kedwell's penalty had ensured that it had only taken nine years to get there, AFC Wimbledon played their first game as a Football League club when they hosted a Fulham XI in a friendly at Kingsmeadow. Despite facing a team fielding several men with Premier League experience, second-half goals from Brett Johnson and new signing Charles Ademino ensured that most of the 1,890 crowd went home happy.

10th July 2002

A crowd of 4,657 packed into Sutton's Gander Green Lane ground to witness the birth of AFC Wimbledon. Former Chelsea player Joe Sheerin, who led the new Dons out, admitted he did not know the names of all his team-mates, but a 4-0 defeat failed to dampen the enthusiasm of supporters. After years of protesting about the destruction of their club, they just wanted the chance, in the words of chairman Kris Stewart, 'to watch some football'.

11th July 2015

Neal Ardley admitted he had been nervous about the age of his young side ahead of the pre-season friendly against Premier League Watford. However, penalties from Callum Kennedy and George Francomb ensured the match ended 2-2. 'I was a bit wary before the game because we had eight players under the age of 22,' the manager said. 'Our boys acquitted themselves really well and I thought defensively, particularly in the first half, we were solid.'

12th July 1965

The club's all-time leading goalscorer, Eddie Reynolds, announced that he would be returning to his native Belfast at the end of the forthcoming campaign. 'I have had some great years at Wimbledon so it will be a wrench to leave,' he was quoted as saying. 'Before I go, I would like to reach 400 goals.' Since making his debut for the Dons in the autumn of 1957, the giant Ulsterman had hit the back of the net 362 times.

13th July 1991

The Dons staged a photoshoot at Selhurst Park ahead of their first campaign domiciled in SE25. Chairman Stanley Reed described the move away from Plough Lane as the latest part of the club's journey of 'many milestones of adventure, progress and well-being'. It was the start of what would be 11 consecutive seasons playing at the historic home of Crystal Palace.

14th July 1959

Just back from England's summer tour of South America, Plough Lane resident Jimmy Greaves presented his next-door neighbour, Eddie Reynolds, with the shirt he had collected from Brazilian ace Didi at the Maracanã Stadium. While the England international was about to prepare for a First Division campaign with Chelsea, the Ulsterman was readying himself to begin the defence of Wimbledon's Isthmian League title.

15th July 1995

The Dons drew 0-0 with Beitar Jerusalem in the third match of their ill-fated participation in the Intertoto Cup. Having just missed out on a place in the UEFA Cup after finishing ninth in the Premier League, the club was compelled to take part and fielded a side including fringe first-teamers and youth players from Manchester United and elsewhere in front of a few hundred fans at Brighton's Goldstone Ground.

16th July 1966

Having finished fifth in their first season at the top level of non-league football, Wimbledon announced their determination to maintain their upward momentum. 'We are keen to get into Division Four despite the fact that we failed to get a single vote at the Football League's AGM,' director Stan Jasper explained. 'We must win the Southern League and Southern League Cup to justify our claim to be the number one club seeking Football League status.'

17th July 2002

Glenn Mulcaire scored AFC Wimbledon's first ever goal, in the club's third match, a friendly at Hayes Lane against Bromley. 'I knew it was going in as soon as I hit it,' 'Trigger' was quoted as saying. 'I could tell by the leverage and the way my knee was over the ball that Glyn Shimell in the Bromley goal was not going to save it.'

18th July 2019

As detailed drawings showing the layout of the new Plough Lane were released, the club announced it wanted to part-fund the build cost through crowdfunding. 'It is a challenge for a fan-owned club to raise finance,' chief executive Joe Palmer said. 'It's perfect for us because it lets us not only reach out directly to the people who matter the most – our own fans – but it also allows those who admire what the club has achieved to be part of the story.'

19th July 1999

Egil Olsen took charge for his first game as Wimbledon manager, a pre-season friendly at Plymouth Argyle. 'When I left Vålerenga I said I would only go to Brazil or Wimbledon,' the former Norway national coach explained. 'It was a joke, but it had truth. Beating Brazil twice, especially in the World Cup, were my most meaningful moments in football. Brazil obviously had superior players, but Norway had a Wimbledon-style game to beat them.'

20th July 2002

Despite losing their fourth friendly in a row, 4-2 at Boreham Wood, Terry Eames, the manager of the new Dons, was in ebullient mood. 'We have seized people's imagination because we are the history and lifeblood of Wimbledon,' he said. 'I've been delighted with the reaction we've had. We've had support from all over the country, from every club. We're starting something new and refreshing and I know the world of football is with us.'

21st July 2007

The Wimbledon Independent Supporters Association issued a statement urging fans to write a response to the latest proposals for Merton's long-term borough plan (LDF). 'The LDF provides a huge opportunity to help us return to the borough – as and when possible – because it sets out planning policy in the borough for the next 15 years. If we can get provision for a stadium included in the final planning guidelines, it could be crucial to getting us back.'

22nd July 1980

Having been relegated back to the Fourth Division the previous May, the Dons' new season opened with a 2-2 draw in a friendly against Chelsea. 'When we were promoted in my first full year in the job, I thought it was down to my brilliant leadership and when we were relegated last May I blamed the players,' manager Dario Gradi explained. 'I have been away in the summer and come back with a more realistic appreciation of my abilities.'

23rd July 2003

Terry Eames said his squad was 'shaping up nicely' as he announced six new signings ahead of the club's second season of Combined Counties League football. 'Our main aim this season is promotion,' the manager said. 'It was all new to us last year and I thought we did excellently in the second half of the season to finish third. But now there can be no excuses and having strengthened our squad we should be up there from the off.'

24th July 2004

Newly promoted to Ryman League Division One, the Dons stunned Conference favourites Barnet by winning a pre-season friendly 3-0. 'He is very professional which is great,' Matt Everard said of new manager Dave Anderson. 'I am very impressed with him, and his approach can only benefit the club. We all believe we can be promoted again this year and I aim to play as many games as possible.'

25th July 2008

A 'What's Happening at Kingsmeadow' feature on the club's website revealed that 1,431 season tickets had been sold ahead of the Dons' first season of Conference South football, good progress was being made in completing the extension to the Main Stand, and the new replica kit had arrived and would be on sale at the 'Meet the Manager' event that evening.

26th July 1997

On a ground where they had secured victory in each of their five previous visits, the Dons beat Bournemouth 2-0 in a pre-season match at Dean Court. Manager of the year Joe Kinnear had kept the vast majority of the squad that had enjoyed so much Premier League and cup success the previous season together and hopes were high that with investment from the club's new Norwegian owners it would be another successful campaign.

27th July 1989

Warming up for their centenary season, an Alan Cork goal was enough for the Dons to beat Swedish club Finnskogaf 1-0 on the first match of a five-game Scandinavian tour. The tragic news of the death of Laurie Cunningham had cast a shadow over the summer, with Terry Gibson saying of his former team-mate, 'He wasn't just a good player; he was a tremendous guy. Some of the things he could do with a football were out of this world.'

28th July 2001

At the start of what proved to be their last season, Wimbledon FC won a practice match at Northampton Town 7-0. On a scorching hot afternoon, a first-half hat-trick from David Connolly, two strikes from Neil Shipperley and goals from Patrick Agyemang and Jobi McAnuff were more than enough for Terry Burton's men to see off the Cobblers at their then six-year-old Sixfields Stadium.

29th July 2011

AFC Wimbledon opened their first season as a Football League club with a League Cup defeat at Crawley Town. Playing a competitive fixture in July for the first time, the Dons twice took the lead, through Luke Moore and Jack Midson, before Matt Tubbs grabbed what proved to be the winner in the 64th minute. Despite Hope Akpan's dismissal, the Red Devils held on to secure victory.

A return to Plough Lane now becomes a reality and first plans are drawn up for what will eventually become the new Dons home.

30th July 2018

Having become the third-longest-serving manager in England when Arsène Wenger left Arsenal, Neal Ardley instigated a major shake-up to prevent the Dons becoming stale. 'Last season shook us up a bit and was not the forward step we wanted,' he said. 'There was a lot we learned that we wanted to change and sometimes you need a bit of a fresh start to do that. I have been at the club more than five and a half years. You can get a bit stale in the job, and I am sure at times the fans get bored of me.'

31st July 1985

The Dons beat West Ham 4-2 in a friendly at Plough Lane. 'I am looking forward to the season,' manager Dave Bassett said. 'Last year was out first in Division Two and if we can find some consistency we should do well. There are no excuses as we now have a year's experience of going to places like Elland Road, Maine Road and St Andrew's. The critics have written us off once again, but I am looking for us to challenge at the top.'

AFC WIMBLEDON

On This Day

AUGUST

1st August 1985

An inspection in the wake of the Bradford stadium fire, which killed 56 people, led to the South Stand at Plough Lane being closed until further notice. Installed in 1923 when it was brought from Clapton Orient's ground in east London, the wooden structure would need major alterations before it could be used to house spectators again.

1st August 1998

In the opening game of the Portsmouth Centenary Tournament, played on a hot afternoon at Fratton Park, the Dons lost 4-3 on penalties to FC Sochaux following a 1-1 draw at the end of 90 minutes. After Genoa rather pooped the party by overcoming the hosts in the second game, Wimbledon beat Alan Ball's side 3-1 in the third-place match the following day.

2nd August 1977

Playing their first match since being elected to the Football League, Billy Holmes was on target as the Dons lost 3-1 to Third Division Colchester United in a Plough Lane friendly. 'Today is just the start – I am sure we can become a First Division club in time,' chairman Ron Noades commented. 'The potential here is fantastic. We aim to become one of the top clubs in London.'

2nd August 2001

The directors of Wimbledon FC announced their intention to move to Milton Keynes to 'ensure the survival of the club'. The response from the Wimbledon Independent Supporters Association was swift. '[Club chairman Charles] Koppel is all too aware that the vast majority of Wimbledon fans are against the scheme,' spokesman Charlie Talbot said. 'He knows how vehement the protests were when this ridiculous scheme was leaked earlier this year.'

3rd August 1968

Twenty-one-year-old John O'Mara scored as the Dons completed their preparations for a new Southern League season with a comfortable 3-0 friendly win at Gravesend. A tall, strong striker who looked uncertain on the ground but excellent in the air, supporters quickly compared him to all-time top scorer Eddie Reynolds. 'I would certainly like to think we had another Eddie on our hands, who wouldn't?' manager Les Henley said. 'But these are early days, and he has a lot to learn. But the potential is there.'

3rd August 2013

Torquay centre-back Aaron Downes scored a stoppage-time equaliser to deny AFC Wimbledon a victory at the start of their third campaign as a Football League club. With six debutants in the side, the new-look Dons looked solid at the back and attacked with pace to create enough chances to have won the game. Neal Ardley's men finally broke the deadlock when a Harry Pell shot from outside the box was deflected into the net by Downes with just three minutes left.

4th August 1970

Police reinforcements were called to Plough Lane as Chelsea supporters in the 3,000 crowd invaded the pitch during a pre-season friendly. Fans climbed the floodlight pylons, got on to the West Bank roof, and mounted the scaffolding on the half-finished Sydney Black Hall. When the game restarted, the Southern League Dons went down to a 5-4 defeat.

4th August 1999

A major survey found Wimbledon to be the 'most efficient' team in the Premier League, once results had been analysed alongside the amount of money spent chasing trophies. 'This is an amazing achievement,' report author Dr Bill Gerrard, of the Leeds University Business School, commented. 'Wimbledon have very few fans, don't own their own ground, regularly sell their best players to bigger clubs, and don't have the history or geography to be a top club. Yet they are consistently competitive.'

5th August 2001

Concerned about reaction to the directors' announcement that the club was set to move to Milton Keynes, manager Terry Burton sounded nervous about how the fans would react during the season. 'It is not an ideal situation for us, and we will have to see what form the demonstrations take,' he said. 'I hope they support the side because with them behind us we have every chance of success.'

5th August 2017

A debut goal from Jimmy Abdou earned a very creditable opening-day point for the Dons at Scunthorpe. Neal Ardley's men came from behind to secure a 1-1 draw that was the least they deserved after completely dominating the second half at Glanford Park. The former Millwall man's excellent strike in the 67th minute threatened to be the platform for a League One win in Lincolnshire, but promotion hopefuls Scunthorpe just managed to cling on.

6th August 2011

Adam Virgo's 85th-minute penalty earned Bristol Rovers a 3-2 win and wrecked AFC Wimbledon's Football League debut. Wearing white in honour of their predecessors who had made their Fourth Division bow back in 1977, the new Dons fluffed their lines in front of the Sky cameras. Having fought back from two goals down to equalise, Brett Johnson's handball cost the Dons dear.

6th August 2021

Having signed seven players in the summer transfer window, Mark Robinson seemed satisfied ahead of a new campaign. 'People don't see the work behind the scenes that goes into it, but we got every first target that we wanted, which was really pleasing,' the Dons' head coach said. 'We knew we were not going to be able to keep Joe Pigott, but we feel we got an awful lot right in the recruitment process – we're very pleased.'

7th August 1971

The Dons drew 2-2 with Orient in a Plough Lane friendly ahead of their Southern League season. 'I hope the supporters will be patient,' new manager Mike Everitt said afterwards. 'I've been pleased with the way the side is shaping up, but it will take us a little time to settle down. There isn't a lot of money around and I have done my best to improve the squad within the constraints of what we can afford.'

7th August 1999

Despite playing for more than 70 minutes with ten men following Dean Blackwell's dismissal, the Dons began their Premier League season with a 3-2 win at Watford. 'The performance was about average,' new manager Egil Olsen said afterwards. 'We like to play the ball long and we are strong in the air. I was proud of the strength and guts of the players.' It proved to be a relegation campaign for both teams.

8th August 2009

An 81st-minute penalty from substitute Jon Main ensured the Dons secured a draw with Luton Town in their first game at Blue Square Premier level. Outplayed for an hour, Terry Brown's men fought back well, and the spot kick was no more than their late pressure deserved. 'I thought the pace of the game was a good yard quicker than what we've been used to, and we did well to match them,' the manager observed.

8th August 2015

Described as a 'reality check' by Neal Ardley, the Dons lost their opening match of the season at home to Plymouth Argyle. 'We need to get the front boys fitter and more dynamic, and we are trying that in training,' the manager said. 'Lyle [Taylor] came in late, Tom [Elliott] has missed a couple of weeks with a back injury and Adebayo [Akinfenwa] normally comes alive when the season starts. We need them, they are important players.'

9th August 1976

Alan Cork played his first game at Plough Lane as his Derby County reserve team lost a pre-season friendly 3-0. He later recalled, 'Before the match our manager told us to "Look out for the number six. He wears a signet ring and will try and hit you with it when he swings his arm." That was Dave Bassett. Within a minute of the kick-off, Roger Connell had elbowed [Derby's former England captain] Roy McFarland in the face. You had to be tough to survive in football in those days.'

9th August 2014

Goals from debutants Matt Tubbs and Sean Rigg were not enough as Shrewsbury Town fought back twice to draw on League Two's opening day at Kingsmeadow. 'It was decent performance, an OK point,' manager Neal Ardley reckoned. 'We have to take all the positives we can from a game against one of the promotion favourites. After the first 20 minutes we were the better team until the last ten minutes. We looked more likely to score.'

10th August 1974

Allen Batsford was in bullish mood after his Southern League side had beaten a full-strength Crystal Palace outfit 1-0 in a pre-season friendly at Plough Lane. 'There is a tremendous setup here with the potential to improve the ground, the team, the facilities, everything,' the new manager explained. 'And that is what we must do ... build right through the club if we are to progress. And if the club wants Football League status, we must consider a reserve and youth team.'

10th August 2002

A fans-led protest urging supporters not to go through the Selhurst Park turnstiles for the opening game of the season between 'Wimbledon' and Gillingham reduced the attendance to 2,476. On the TV, there was a live feed from Garth Crooks at the ground. He said, 'The football was an irrelevance. The result today was clear: AFC Wimbledon 1, Wimbledon FC 0.'

11th August 2001

Fans released hundreds of black balloons to signal the death of the club as a new First Division campaign began at Selhurst Park. With chairman Charles Koppel having announced plans to relocate the club to Milton Keynes, a 3-1 victory over Birmingham City, courtesy of goals from debutants Neil Shipperley and David Connolly, was almost forgotten amid the chants of 'We want Koppel out' and banners reading 'MK – NO WAY'.

11th August 2010

A record crowd at Eastbourne Borough's Priory Lane ground saw the Dons lose their first away fixture in the Blue Square Premier. A wonderful 25-yard drive from former Wimbledon FC apprentice Neil Jenkins in the 50th minute proved to be the winner and, although the visitors played with more urgency in the final half an hour, they did not have the firepower to overcome a resolute home defence.

12th August 2000

Playing their first match outside the top flight for 14 years, the Dons were not able to break down a stubborn Tranmere rearguard at Selhurst Park. Despite creating numerous chances, the absence of John Hartson and Jason Euell proved costly as Wimbledon dominated most of the play but could not make their superiority tell even after Sean Flynn was dismissed for the visitors. 'I was reasonably happy with the performance, if not the result,' manager Terry Burton said.

12th August 2008

Late goals from Elliott Godfrey and Luke Garrard allowed the Dons to come from behind and beat Thurrock 2-1 in the Conference South. 'We were knocking on the door almost throughout the second half,' manager Terry Brown said. 'I'd like to say a big "thank you" to you the supporters who stayed with us and didn't get too frustrated at what will be several teams' tactics this year. I can't say it will always have such a pleasant outcome.'

13th August 1983

After the Dons had drawn a pre-season friendly 2-2 against Charlton Athletic, manager Dave Bassett assessed his just-promoted side's prospects. 'This time we want to stay up,' he said. 'I think we have more chance because almost all our current players experienced Third Division football on our last visit. 'We won't be looking just for survival; we want to be promoted. But we will need a little luck – not bundles of it, just our fair share.'

13th August 2011

Rashid Yussuff struck a spectacular second-half goal in a 2-1 victory at Dagenham to earn AFC Wimbledon their first Football League win. After falling behind to Jon Nurse's early effort, the Dons were awarded a penalty on 37 minutes and Luke Moore made no mistake from the spot. Victory was secured just before the hour when midfielder Yussuff was allowed to advance from midfield unchallenged and he thundered home a fierce shot from 25 yards out.

14th August 1973

The just-appointed Dick Graham watched from the stands as Ian Cooke's lone goal was enough to beat big-spending Dover in a Southern League match at Plough Lane. 'I have got to get to know the strengths and characters of my players, but you would have to be blind not to see that we are short up front,' the new manager commented. 'Goalscoring is something that you cannot coach into a player, and I will need to look outside the club.'

14th August 2004

The Dave Anderson era got off to a perfect start as his Ryman League Division One side cruised to an opening-day win. 'When Ashford went ahead early on, I realised how big a job I had taken on,' the manager recalled. 'You could have heard a pin drop. It was a step up for me and the players. Most of them were not used to playing in front of such big crowds. I needn't have worried. Two minutes later Richard Butler equalised, and we were away.'

15th August 1987

The opening-day reunion with former manager Dave Bassett proved a feisty one as the Dons slipped to defeat at Watford. But for the brilliance of goalkeeper Dave Beasant – a man new boss Bobby Gould had refused to sell during the summer – the loss would have been heavier. 'It may have been a good performance for me personally, but I am sick because we have lost,' the goalkeeper told reporters. 'We have been working hard in training, but it seems that we still have more to do.'

15th August 1998

Manager Joe Kinnear was in bullish mood at a press conference after his team had beaten the expensively assembled Tottenham Hotspur side 3-1 on the opening day of the Premier League season. 'Where are they? All the people who said we would go down? One, two, three, there are about nine of you in here,' he began. 'I knew that if we attacked with pace, we could punish them [Spurs]. We are in great shape. When I can get my best side out, we can match anyone.'

16th August 2003

Goals from Lee Sidwell and Matt Everard gave the Dons an opening-day Combined Counties League win at Feltham. 'The team knows each other now, after a year together, and we have to win the league this season,' striker Kevin Cooper said. 'Last year we started badly but we had some players who would not get near the team now. I firmly believe we will come top of the league and there will be some entertainment for our supporters along the way.'

16th August 2014

Luton's first Football League match at home since 2009 ended in disappointment as Matt Tubbs's goal earned the Dons a 1-0 League Two win at Kenilworth Road. 'Tubbs's finish was different class,' manager Neal Ardley commented. 'Second half, I thought we had enough chances to score four. All in all, it was a very good day for us. There won't be many teams who come here and beat this lot.'

17th August 1974

A penalty and Selwyn Rice's sending-off combined to blight the start of the Allen Batsford era. 'Even with ten men we still created chances and could have scored a couple of goals,' the new manager commented at the end. 'I was upset about the sending-off at the time but, having reflected, the referee was quite right to dismiss Rice as he punched him.'

17th August 2002

Nearly 2,500 fans basked in the sun as the new Dons kicked off their Combined Counties League campaign with a 2-1 win at Sandhurst Town. 'After all the hard work from everyone to overcome the nightmare of May 28th, I felt a few tears in my eyes when we kicked off today,' chairman Kris Stewart said. 'That was our team out there today, playing for us and playing for points. It was a great day out and I hope there are many more to come.'

18th August 1962

Eddie Reynolds was on target as the champion Dons opened their season by losing 3-1 to a Rest of the League XI in SW19. It was Wimbledon's only warm-up game at the start of a glorious campaign that saw the club retain their Isthmian League title, claim their first Football League scalp by knocking Colchester United out of the FA Cup and add the FA Amateur Cup to the Plough Lane trophy cabinet.

18th August 1987

'We went into the game as underdogs but came out as bulldogs,' manager Bobby Gould said after his team had secured a 1-1 draw with champions Everton in his first home league match in charge of the Dons. 'It's never easy coming here,' visiting boss Colin Harvey responded. 'I think Wimbledon will do well again this year. They work really hard and play to their strengths.'

19th August 1964

Producing one of the most remarkable comebacks in their long history, the Dons came from 4-0 down at the interval to win a pre-season friendly at Josephs Road. Facing Southern Premier League opposition in Guildford City, the Division One new boys hit back thanks to two goals from Paul Hodges and a hat-trick from Eddie Reynolds. It augured well for the club's first season of semi-professional football.

19th August 1989

FA Cup Final hero Dave Beasant returned to Plough Lane with his newly promoted Chelsea team and produced several outstanding saves to help his side earn an opening-day victory. 'I could not believe how difficult Wimbledon were to play against,' the goalkeeper said. 'They put us under so much pressure and at times it was just a case of holding on. I really enjoyed the day, especially the save against Corkie. I told him before the game that he was not going to score.'

20th August 1977

Allen Batsford said his team were 'disgraceful' and 'nowhere near aggressive enough' as the Dons' inaugural Fourth Division fixture ended in a 3-3 draw with Halifax Town. Having gone in at half-time a goal down, Jeff Bryant scored the club's first Football League goal six minutes after the restart and further strikes from John Leslie and Roger Connell saw the hosts lead 3-2 with just moments left before a late equaliser soured the mood at Plough Lane.

20th August 1988

John Aldridge gained a modicum of revenge for the bitter disappointment of missing his FA Cup Final penalty by scoring in both halves to ensure Liverpool won the Charity Shield by beating the Dons 2-1 at Wembley. Featuring just six men who had lined up against the league champions in May, manager Bobby Gould fielded an unfamiliar side for the traditional season-opener. 'I thought we did well in the circumstances,' Gould said.

21st August 1965

Facing the toughest possible start to life in the Southern League Premier Division, the Dons were narrowly beaten at champions Weymouth. The visiting defence, marshalled superbly by Tommy McCready in the absence of Roy Law, played well under severe pressure at the Rec but eventually conceded a 65th-minute winning goal when winger Geoff Tizard found enough space to volley the ball home at Mike Kelly's near post.

21st August 2007

Richard Jolly and Daniel Webb scored as the Dons registered a Ryman Premier League win at Wealdstone. 'I told the players after the match that the majority of the games this season are going to be like that – not great to watch but requiring a lot of hard work,' manager Dave Anderson said. 'We changed our formation slightly in the second half and I thought we looked far more effective, but we were never able to kill the game off.'

22nd August 1964

The biggest Southern League Division One crowd of the day – 3,432 – saw the Dons do everything but score as they made their semi-professional debut against Poole Town at Plough Lane. 'We didn't meet a better side in the First Division last season,' Poole boss Doug Millward admitted. 'Wimbledon will win a lot of matches and may well gain promotion at the first attempt.'

22nd August 2020

Having agreed to play their games at Loftus Road until the construction of their new Plough Lane stadium was completed, the Dons had an early taste of their temporary home as they lost a pre-season friendly 3-0 against landlords Queens Park Rangers. With the previous campaign having been cut short due to the Covid-19 pandemic, both teams were keen to get back in action before the competitive games started again.

23rd August 1985

Described by the *Sunday Mirror* as 'the worst team ever to play in the First Division', the Dons went down 3-1 as they made their top-flight debut at Manchester City. 'The way they play will upset a lot of teams,' home boss Billy McNeil commented, 'they certainly upset me.' His opposite number, Dave Bassett, responded, 'We feel we should have got something from the game but it's better coming here than playing Rochdale isn't it.'

23rd August 2005

Richard Butler scored two second-half goals to help the Dons to a 2-0 midweek Ryman Premier League victory at Maldon Town. 'Butler was unbelievable,' manager Dave Anderson said. 'If I'd been a Football League manager watching this game, I'd have been straight on the phone to sign him up. He has progressed as a player since we signed him a year ago and developed in every avenue.'

24th August 1976

Forced by injuries and suspensions to field six newcomers in losing the first leg 2-0 at Romford, the Dons eventually levelled the aggregate score in the second leg of a Southern League Cup tie at Plough Lane. With the rules not allowing extra time, it meant a replay. 'At one point I thought we had run out of time,' a relieved Allen Batsford commented afterwards. 'But we could have been three or four up at half-time.'

24th August 1991

Goals from Robbie Earle and John Fashanu ensured the Dons beat West Ham 2-0 at their new home in SE25. 'We have the scope at Selhurst Park to become one of the major powers in football, especially with the advent of the likely super league,' owner Sam Hammam said. 'We have constantly surprised people, season after season, and I think it is time people started expecting Wimbledon to be successful. We have some top-quality players, and the club will continue to do well.'

25th August 1984

The sight of the biggest crowd at Plough Lane since the club joined the Football League – 8,365 – failed to impress every observer as the Dons opened their first Second Division season with a 2-2 draw against promotion favourites Manchester City. 'The second coming might struggle to rope in 10,000 in Wimbledon,' the man from the *Sunday Times* joked. 'City, in their glory days, would have got that number to watch [Maine Road legend] Frannie Lee walk his dog.'

25th August 2012

Having conceded six goals at Burton in midweek, the Dons were beaten 5-1 at Bradford City. 'It feels like it has been the longest week of my life,' shell-shocked manager Terry Brown admitted. 'Here and on Tuesday we've conceded three goals in the first 20 minutes. We will go out and work hard on the training ground. It is up to me to instil a little bit of confidence in them.'

26th August 2000

After failing to find the net in their opening two First Division fixtures, the return of John Hartson failed to provide the spark as the Dons drew 0-0 at Watford. 'More than anything I want to get back to how I was playing at West Ham when I was scoring 25 goals a season,' the striker said. 'I had a bad year when there were one or two problems with injuries and other things, now I am right mentally again.'

26th August 2002

A Matt Everard-inspired Ash United gave the large travelling army a reality check as three late goals sent the Dons crashing to Combined Counties League defeat at Shawfield Road. Keith Ward's dismissal was a turning point, but home assistant boss Jamie Horton poured cold water on the visitors' promotion hopes when he said, 'To be honest, apart from Cooper and Sheerin up front, I don't think any of their players would get into our side.'

27th August 1963

Bone-jarring tackles, petty fouls and a goalkeeper being carried off on a stretcher marred the much-anticipated clash between the previous season's Athenian and Isthmian League champions. With Enfield joining the Isthmian ranks and keen to stop the Dons securing a hat-trick of titles, Les Henley's team showed a steely determination in firing home three unanswered goals to get their season off to a winning start.

27th August 1983

Hoping it would be third time lucky after their two previous seasons in the Third Division had ended in failure, the Dons opened the new campaign with a 2-0 defeat at Bolton. 'If we had gone in two up at half-time it would have reflected the balance of play,' manager Dave Bassett commented. 'Finishing was not a problem I expected to have after all the goals we scored last season but Alan Cork flies back from Sweden later this week and will be available next Saturday.'

28th August 1990

A desperately poor-quality encounter at Queens Park Rangers was settled in the Dons' favour when Hans Segers launched a huge kick downfield and John Fashanu headed it over the flat-footed home goalkeeper Tony Roberts for the only goal. 'Every match he is in the shop window and thinks Real Madrid are watching him,' manager Ray Harford said of his unsettled striker. 'It is not difficult to motivate him. I want him to stay at the club for life – he leads the line so well.'

28th August 2010

Terry Brown's boys went to the top of the Blue Square Premier table after a thrilling victory at Eastbourne Borough. Leading 2-0 after an hour, the Dons relaxed, allowing the hosts to level, before a brilliant finale in which Sam Hatton released Danny Kedwell to round goalkeeper Banks and fire home a 90th-minute winner. 'I hope our players learned something today,' the relieved manager commented. 'Never take anything for granted.'

29th August 1981

Dave Bassett's first full season in charge began with a 4-1 defeat at Swindon Town's County Ground. 'On another day they might have beaten us,' Robins boss John Trollope admitted afterwards. 'It was pleasing for football the way they came at us.' 'Disappointed but not despondent,' was the Dons boss's post-match verdict. 'The scoreline says we've been stuffed but it was nothing like that really.'

29th August 1989

A blood-and-thunder local top-flight derby at Plough Lane saw the Dons draw 2-2 with Millwall. The dismissal of Eric Young took the headlines as the hosts had to settle for a point following Tony Cascarino's late goal. 'There were a lot of things that the referee didn't see that Wimbledon got away with,' Lions boss John Doherty commented. 'It is very difficult when other teams are bent on confrontation.'

30th August 1958

Ex-Woking men Geoff Hamm and Phil Ledger helped the Dons to defeat their old club in an Isthmian League thriller at Plough Lane. Midfielder Hamm pulled the strings as the hosts moved into a 5-2 lead by the 55th minute before the man the FA Amateur Cup holders had deemed surplus to requirements, goalkeeper Ledger, came into his own. He produced a series of fine saves, including one from the spot, as Wimbledon, with 21-year-old Roy Law making his debut, held on to win 5-4.

30th August 1986

Desperate defending allowed the Dons to protect the lead given to them by Alan Cork's first-half goal and secure their second First Division win in four days, with victory over Leicester City. 'We were totally drained at the end,' Dave Bassett said. 'It was organised chaos out there, but we managed to hang on.' Earlier in the week the manager had been presented with the inaugural Bernard Joy Memorial Award after guiding his club through the divisions to reach the top flight.

31st August 2009

The Dons moved up to third in the Blue Square Premier table after an August Bank Holiday victory at Grays Athletic. 'After seven games at this level, I feel we have nothing to fear,' manager Terry Brown commented. 'We will now look to build on this good start and play more football in the future.'

31st August 2014

First-half goals from Harry Pell and Michael Smith ensured a 2-0 victory over high-flying Fleetwood Town and moved the Dons up to fourth in the League Two table. 'That was probably our best display since I joined the club. We put in a proper team performance – from minute one through to minute 90,' delighted manager Neal Ardley reflected afterwards. 'I thought Michael Smith was unplayable. He gave them a really, really tough time.'

AFC WIMBLEDON
On This Day

SEPTEMBER

1st September 1934

Nearly 5,000 fans watched from the newly concreted West Bank at Plough Lane as the Dons put seven goals past Ilford. Ironically, it was only after Dellow had hit the bar for the visitors that Wimbledon got into their stride, and they were five up at the interval. W.W. 'Doc' Dowden completed his hat-trick in the second half as the hosts made it two wins from two games at the start of what would prove a title-winning Isthmian League campaign.

1st September 2020

Adam Roscrow bagged his first Dons goal and Terell Thomas added another in an impressive victory over Charlton Athletic in the EFL Trophy. Playing their first home game at Loftus Road at the start of a Covid-delayed season, Wimbledon dominated for long spells. 'It was really pleasing that a lot of stuff came together and towards the end it looked like the boys were enjoying the experience,' manager Glyn Hodges said.

2nd September 1967

Patience was rewarded when the totally dominant Dons finally breached the Hastings United defence to record a Southern League Premier Division victory at the Pilot Field. The just-promoted hosts had lost every one of their opening four games of the season and adopted an ultra-cautious approach against Les Henley's title hopefuls.

2nd September 1986

Dennis Wise's first league goal was enough to beat Charlton Athletic and leave the Dons top of the First Division table. There were just three minutes of normal time remaining when the 19-year-old Southampton reject was on hand to bundle the ball home from close range after Jones had blocked John Fashanu's effort. 'All the experts wrote them off [before the start of the season],' said Addicks boss Lennie Lawrence, 'but I can tell you it takes some effort and commitment to match them.'

3rd September 1985

Fewer than 2,400 people turned out to watch as a Paul Fishenden goal proved enough for the Dons to beat Barnsley and move up to second place in the Second Division. One of five players from the club's youth system in the starting line-up, the youngster got the important goal in the opening quarter. 'We let them off the hook in the first half and it meant we had to live dangerously after that,' manager Dave Bassett commented. 'It should have been all over at the interval.'

3rd September 2011

Christian Jolley's injury-time winner helped the Dons beat Port Vale 3-2 for their first League Two home win. 'How on earth we went in at half-time 1-0 up I will never know,' manager Terry Brown admitted. 'They should have been three or four up because we were not at the races. It was our day and Lady Luck was certainly on our side. My players showed tremendous character to go on and win having lost the lead twice.'

4th September 1976

The Dons were still without a win or even a goal after their third Southern League game of the season ended in defeat at Rockingham Road. Kettering skipper Billy Kellock scored the only goal of the game in the 81st minute as Wimbledon's hopes of a third successive title took another blow. 'We played well,' manager Allen Batsford claimed. 'If we had taken our chances, we could have come away with a 3-1 win. Once we have got a few goals under our belts we shall start to go.'

4th September 2021

The Dons downed high-flying Oxford United as their fine League One start under coach Mark Robinson continued with a 3-1 win at Plough Lane. Behind at the break, Jack Rudoni's brace and a goal from Will Nightingale turned the game around. 'You dream about days like that,' Robinson said. 'The atmosphere was incredible, and the second-half performance was pleasing.'

5th September 1992

The Dons recorded their first Premier League win at the seventh attempt after shooting down title favourites Arsenal. Wimbledon refused to allow their illustrious opponents to set the pace and the score was locked at 2-2 when John Fashanu's aggressive style caused panic in the Gunners' back line late on and, when the ball ran loose, Robbie Earle was on hand to gleefully slam home the winner.

5th September 2014

An Ade Azeez goal deep in stoppage time ensured the Dons made the long journey home from Carlisle with a point following a 4-4 draw. 'It's a point gained, but we have got to learn,' manager Neal Ardley said as his side's shaky start to the new campaign continued. 'League Two is an unforgiving place and I give us credit for digging in. They fought incredibly hard and at 4-2 deserved to be in front but my boys fought well and got their reward.'

6th September 1986

Watford and England star John Barnes praised the Dons after their 1-0 victory at Vicarage Road had consolidated their position at the top of the First Division. 'We had a lot of criticism for our style, and it didn't bother us,' he said. 'There's more to them than just kick-and-rush. They beat us tactically by cutting off all our channels to attack with five men at the back who would not be drawn out. They deserve all they get. They are hard for other teams to stop – it is very hard to stop a bulldozer.'

6th September 2003

Three up in ten minutes, the Dons totally dominated Westfield in the first qualifying round of the FA Vase and ended up as 7-0 winners. Using their wingers to torment the full-backs in a match played at Woking's Kingfield ground, Wimbledon controlled the game and scored almost at will. 'We really came out firing today,' hat-trick hero Kevin Cooper said afterwards. 'The wide boys were superb and the amount of chances they created was unreal.'

7th September 1965

Already two goals down from the first leg of a Southern League Cup tie, a pitiful Sittingbourne team came to Plough Lane like lambs to the slaughter. The goal-hungry Dons forwards duly reached double figures as they feasted on some amateurish defending. When the fifth strike went in soon after half-time, a visiting supporter shouted, 'Come on 'Bourne – all you need is seven quick goals.' At 9-0, the home fans began chanting, 'We want ten!' and Brian Keats duly obliged.

7th September 1991

A pitiful First Division attendance of just 3,231 saw the Dons easily overcome a desperately poor Luton Town side in the Selhurst Park sun. Andy Clarke put Wimbledon ahead before Vaughan Ryan added two more after the break. 'It felt like a practice match with such a large stadium and such a small crowd,' manager Ray Harford commented. 'The gates weren't much better at Plough Lane, but it was such an intimate ground you always heard the fans.'

8th September 1979

Previously unbeaten Blackburn Rovers came a cropper at Plough Lane as the Dons recorded their first Third Division victory. Having stressed the importance of battling for every ball, manager Dario Gradi must have been delighted when his side's wholehearted display was capped with Ray Knowles's winner with just over a quarter of an hour remaining. The only black mark was a red card for Tommy Cunningham, shown after he headbutted Stuart Parker five minutes from time.

8th September 2018

Joe Pigott's fifth goal of the season was enough to earn the Dons a 1-0 win over Gillingham, their first league victory since the opening day of the campaign. 'It was an all-round team performance,' manager Neal Ardley said. 'Tom Soares and Liam Trotter dominated the midfield and the back four were excellent. We deserved the win and now we have to make sure we take all those qualities into next week and build some momentum.'

9th September 1995

Responding brilliantly after Vinnie Jones was sent off in the 25th minute, the ten-man Dons took the lead against Liverpool and then held on for more than an hour to record a famous Premier League victory. 'We've seen the video and we don't know why the ref sent Jones off,' manager Joe Kinnear said. 'It is a shame because that is what will make all the headlines, but the lads have done it again haven't they? Other sides would have caved in under that sort of pressure.'

9th September 1998

Three down by the 27th minute at Upton Park, the Dons hit back to shock West Ham with a 4-3 victory. 'That's the best comeback away from home that I have been involved in my ten years at the club,' manager Joe Kinnear said. 'It was never-say-die. I told them at half-time that if we kept attacking, they might cave in. Carl Leaburn was magnificent. He won everything in the air and frightened the life out of them.'

10th September 1960

With skipper Jim Wright missing through injury, 2,600 fans saw the Dons put five past their local Isthmian League rivals Woking to advance to the second qualifying round of the FA Cup. After a completely one-sided first half, Wimbledon finally made their superiority pay with goals from their deadly duo of Eddie Reynolds and Brian Martin and a fine strike from Bobby Ardrey. The Cards then pulled one back before Joe Wallis and that man Reynolds gave the scoreline a flattering look.

10th September 1966

Despite being badly injured by a first-half tackle, David Hyde stayed on the pitch to mastermind the Dons' 3-0 Southern League Premier Division win over Hillingdon Borough. 'I felt the boys were right on top and bringing on [substitute] Dave Willis would have really weakened our attacking play,' manager Les Henley explained at the end. 'Hyde was badly bruised but nothing was broken so I decided to keep him on, and it paid off.'

11th September 1971

The club made national newspaper headlines after Mike Everitt refused to appoint Elaine New to the post of team physiotherapist. Despite being the only applicant, the 26-year-old nurse from Colliers Wood was turned down. 'I just couldn't engage her,' the manager explained. 'Psychologically she would have upset my players and I hate to think how their wives would have reacted if they had claimed to have had a groin strain.'

11th September 1993

A Lawrie Sanchez goal was enough to beat Norwich City and leave the Dons fifth in the Premier League. 'I don't think we've necessarily got the consistency to win the league, but I don't see why we cannot win one of the cups and qualify for Europe that way,' John Fashanu commented. 'We play beautiful football as well as some physical stuff and I don't think Europe would ever have seen a team like Wimbledon if we got there. They are unlikely to see a team like us afterwards either!'

12th September 1964

A weekend on the Kent coast designed to boost squad morale turned sour as the ten-man Dons surrendered their unbeaten Southern League Division One record at Ramsgate after John Martin was stretchered off with a broken leg in the 20th minute. With an overnight hotel stay and a Sunday morning golf tournament ahead, Wimbledon battled hard but, with no substitute allowed, the hosts went on to claim a 2-1 victory.

12th September 1970

Alan Burton was forced off with a broken collarbone as the Dons slumped to their third defeat in four Southern League matches, at previously winless Telford United. Player-coach Ron Flowers, a former England international, put the hosts ahead in the early stages and by full time his charges had scored three more. 'I think our league position is misleading,' manager Les Henley said. 'We have played some good football in our last two games, and we could have won them both.'

13th September 1983

The Dons overcame a one-goal deficit from the first leg of their League Cup tie against Southend to win 6-4 after extra time and advance into the second round. Alan Cork, Steve Ketteridge, Steve Galliers, Stewart Evans and Glyn Hodges were all on the scoresheet on a memorable night in SW19. But Shrimpers boss Peter Morris could not resist a swipe about the hosts' 'long ball' style of play. 'No wonder the Plough Lane pitch is in mint condition,' he said. 'The ball's never on it.'

13th September 2008

Twenty-five-year-old Danny Kedwell came off the bench for his debut as the Dons beat Maidenhead United 3-1 to keep up with the Conference South pace-setters. 'You want to make an instant impact and score but hopefully the supporters will have liked what they saw,' the new striker commented. 'I always give my all even if I don't score. I hope to form a partnership with Jon Main that will bring us the goals to get us out of this division.'

14th September 1974

One down after four minutes of an FA Cup first qualifying-round tie at Bracknell Town, the Dons recovered as a three-goal burst gave them a comfortable win. It was to be seven rounds, eight matches and 766 minutes before Dickie Guy conceded again. Even then, it took a deflected goal from First Division champions Leeds United in the fourth-round proper replay at Selhurst Park for the tally clerk in London's West India Docks to finally be beaten.

14th September 2004

Looking to extend their Ryman League Division One winning run to eight games, the Dons were hugely frustrated as Leatherhead hit back with two late goals to snatch a draw. 'We had our best 80 minutes of the season and then our worst ten,' manager Dave Anderson said. 'Conceding two goals inside a minute should not happen at any level. They put three up front and we did not cope – it was unprofessional. Leatherhead simply did not give up and good luck to them.'

15th September 1984

Goals from Glyn Hodges and Kevin Gage helped the Dons win 2-1 at second-placed Shrewsbury Town, Wimbledon's inaugural Second Division victory. 'Getting our first away win has done us a power of good,' manager Dave Bassett said. 'It gives us a bit of confidence and something to build on. I thought [Dave] Beasant was exceptional in goal when they came at us in the second half.'

15th September 2012

Terry Brown's time as manager of the Dons was drawing to a close after defeat at home to Rochdale left his League Two side in 21st place following a disastrous start to the campaign. The visitors were 2-0 up at half-time and Wimbledon's cause was not helped when Jack Midson was sent off for violent conduct after 24 minutes. Luke Moore pulled one back late on but with the Dons Trust board having recently issued a vote of support, many feared for Brown's future.

16th September 1950

Harry Stannard scored six times as the Dons beat the Guildford Pinks 9-3 in an FA Cup preliminary-round match at Plough Lane. The game was so one-sided as to be embarrassing and Wimbledon were leading 9-0 with half an hour to play. Easing off in the closing minutes, the hosts allowed the Surrey League Pinks to score three late, consolation goals.

16th September 2017

Kwesi Appiah's early strike was enough for the Dons to defeat League One promotion favourites Blackburn Rovers 1-0 at Ewood Park. 'Full marks to Wimbledon because they managed to nick a goal and defend it well for the majority of the game,' Rovers boss Tony Mowbray said. 'We have to be better in these situations. We became undisciplined in the last 20 minutes and started hitting long balls instead of playing it wide. That is the way to break down a massed defence.'

17th September 1988

Still in turmoil after the behind-the-scenes machinations in the wake of their Wembley success in May, the Dons were completely outclassed by newly promoted Middlesbrough at Ayresome Park. The home fans chanted derisively, 'How d'you win the FA Cup?' as Gary Hamilton's winner left the visitors in 20th place in the early First Division table. 'We are not worried at the moment,' John Fashanu was quoted as saying. 'We have had a lot of chances, but we just haven't taken them.'

17th September 2016

Late goals from Dominic Poleon and substitute Tyrone Barnett gave the Dons a League One victory at Charlton Athletic. 'It is a cruel game sometimes,' Addicks boss Russell Slade said. 'We've had 12 opportunities and only scored once, Wimbledon had two and scored both. Fair play to them because they stayed in the game and at 1-0, they always had a chance, but we have let ourselves down.'

18th September 1999

Making what turned out to be their last visit to Old Trafford, the Dons led for nearly an hour before Jordi Cruyff equalised to force a 1-1 draw. Walid Badir scored his first Premier League goal when Carl Cort cut the ball back in the 16th minute and the hosts produced precious little in the way of clear-cut chances until the Dutchman rounded Sullivan to level with 16 minutes remaining. 'They had more chances, but we had the big chances,' manager Egil Olsen claimed.

18th September 2012

A freak goal, scored when a clearance hit Torquay's Rene Howe on the backside and bounced into the net, ended Terry Brown's time as the Dons' boss. A poor start to the campaign meant the man who had led the club into the Football League was sacked the following morning. 'It is difficult to explain just how phenomenal Terry is and what he means to everyone here at the club,' midfielder Steven Gregory said. 'He is like a father figure to me.'

19th September 2015

After scoring a rare goal in the Dons' 2-1 League Two victory over Notts County, veteran Dannie Bulman said he was 'happy just to be involved'. In his 17th season as a professional, the midfielder revealed that some of the squad called him 'Dad' and that he did not want to attempt a sliding goal celebration in case he pulled a muscle. 'I think we have a squad here capable of making the play-off places and I want to be part of it,' he added.

19th September 2020

Two late goals earned Plymouth Argyle a thrilling 4-4 draw against the Dons in a helter-skelter encounter at Loftus Road. 'It was not good enough and I'm really disappointed,' said manager Glyn Hodges. 'We keep saying we have to learn, but we are trying to build a winning mentality, of expecting to win our home games. At 4-2, I was thinking we had been lucky because they had caused us problems, but we had got our noses in front. Unfortunately, we couldn't see it through.'

20th September 1952

A Plough Lane crowd of 5,166 saw Wimbledon sew up their Isthmian League clash with Barking inside the first quarter of the game before going on to register an 8-0 win. Two from Harry Stannard and another from Freddie Gauntlett meant the Dons were three up by the midpoint of the first half. After the break, Stannard took his personal tally to four and there were also goals for Reg Marsh and future England cricket coach Mickey Stewart.

20th September 1993

Robbie Earle's second-half goal was enough for the fifth-placed Dons to beat Manchester City and record their third successive Premier League victory. 'We should have won by more,' manager Joe Kinnear reckoned. 'These are heady days. My team are a special bunch of players, and they are the most committed team I have ever worked with in my time in football. The atmosphere inside the dressing room is electric. They're on fire, ready to explode and I would like to keep them buzzing.'

21st September 1963

As the first team registered a 1-0 home victory over a Wycombe Wanderers side that had now lost on seven of their previous eight Isthmian League visits to Plough Lane, in east London a star was born. A youngster called Ian Cooke scored his first goal for the club as the reserves visited Leytonstone. It was noted that the 18-year-old had only taken up football since leaving the rugby-playing Emmanuel School in the summer. He was predicted to have a great future in the game.

21st September 2013

A goal down to ten-man Burton Albion at the break, the Dons stormed back to win a League Two encounter with goals from Michael Smith, Jack Midson and Andy Frampton. 'We came in at half-time and I told them I'd rather lose the game 2-0 or 3-0 than lose it 1-0 when you're at home and playing against ten men,' manager Neal Ardley said. 'So, we went for some pace down the wings, and they carried the plan out to the letter in that second half.'

22nd September 2001

Despite playing for the whole of the second half with ten men, a goal from substitute Neil Shipperley five minutes into added time allowed the Dons to emerge from a First Division trip to West Bromwich Albion victorious. When David Connolly was dismissed for incurring his second yellow card after kicking the ball away in the 40th minute the visitors defended stoutly. 'We needed to dig in and work hard,' manager Terry Burton said. 'I thought all my players were excellent.'

22nd September 2007

Manager Terry Brown admitted that he had still not got the balance of the side right after the Dons' stuttering Ryman League draw at Margate had left them in 14th place. 'We've got to be more professional if we want to go up,' defender Jake Leberl said. 'We've been giving away too many silly goals and that is a worry. If you look at the teams that won non-league titles last year, they were not pretty sides. We need to be more solid as a team.'

23rd September 1978

A stunning strike from Alan Cork allowed the Dons to leapfrog leaders Reading and go top of the Fourth Division. Fielding both Gary Peters and Lawrie Sanchez in their line-up, the Royals saw their unbeaten run come to an end when teenage striker Cork fired home a drive from outside the box with less than 20 minutes remaining. 'I had a bet that I would score 15 goals this season, but it looks like I will hit that mark by Christmas,' the goalscoring sensation commented.

23rd September 2010

Late goals from Sam Hatton and Danny Kedwell saw the Dons come from behind to beat the expensively assembled Crawley Town and go top of the Blue Square Premier. 'I am already at the best club in this division so why would I want to move?' Kedwell commented in response to questions about the Red Devils' attempts to sign him. 'Every striker is out to get the golden boot, but I think it is my year.'

24th September 1977

There were relieved smiles all round Plough Lane as two goals in three first-half minutes – the second from debutant Phil Summerill – produced the Dons' first Fourth Division victory. Visitors Northampton Town were rarely in the game and the hosts could easily have added to their advantage in the second half. 'I knew a win would come sooner or later,' jubilant manager Allen Batsford said at the end.

24th September 1994

Signed from Rochdale for £200,000, Alan Reeves marked QPR's Les Ferdinand out of the game before getting forward to head a 48th-minute winner at Loftus Road. 'Alan has a terrific appetite for the game and can play with both feet – rare for a centre-back,' manager Joe Kinnear said. 'I don't watch Premier League players because I cannot afford them, so I go to the corner shop rather than Harrods.'

25th September 1965

Playing their first season of Southern League Premier Division football, two Eddie Reynolds goals gave the Dons a 2-1 victory at Cheltenham Town and lifted them out of the relegation places. After winning just once in their opening six matches, the Whaddon Road triumph served to kick-start Wimbledon's season and, by the end of November, an eight-game unbeaten run had taken Les Henley's men to the top of the league.

25th September 1971

Injured player-manager Mike Everitt watched from the sidelines as his team completed their sixth successive victory and moved up to second in the Southern League table. Twice behind, the visitors finally overcame Bath's unbeaten home record when the excellent Ian Cooke made the score 3-2 with just two minutes to go. 'Don't expect too much too soon. We are still a work in progress,' said a wary Everitt after the travelling fans chanted about winning the league.

26th September 1981

A miserable afternoon in the West Midlands saw the Dons lose the game and leading scorer Alan Cork at a wet and windy Walsall. Cork broke his leg in a 72nd-minute collision with home goalkeeper Ron Green and, just three minutes later, Don Penn pounced to score the winner. 'It is a big blow for him and the club,' manager Dave Bassett commented. 'It is a serious break and I have written him off for the rest of the season.'

26th September 2006

After going one down in the 80th minute at Ashford Town (Middx), the Dons hit back with two late goals to secure three Ryman League points. 'That was all about team spirit,' manager Dave Anderson reckoned. 'When they got their goal, I feared the worst, but the team just kept going. We got the penalty from a well-worked move, and we got our reward for keeping going when Steve Wales came up with the winner.'

27th September 1975

In terrible conditions, the Dons maintained their flying start to their Southern League campaign by taking two points off Telford United. Driving rain and a strong wind meant Wimbledon did well to put so many dangerous attacks together and the pressure told as they scored three second-half goals. 'I thought we played quite well considering what it was like out there,' said manager Allen Batsford. The result left the defending champions four points clear at the top of the table.

27th September 1980

John Leslie celebrated the signing of a new three-year contract by scoring the winner in a Fourth Division game at Halifax Town. A dour contest was nearing its conclusion when debutant Dave Hubbick crossed the ball and the club's longest-serving player fired the ball home from inside the area. Seventeen-year-old Glyn Hodges became the second newcomer to be introduced at The Shay when he came on as a substitute with ten minutes left.

28th September 1985

Stewart Evans was the hero as his two goals helped the Dons beat Second Division promotion favourites Charlton Athletic at Plough Lane. 'The first one went in off my knee and I scored the second from about six inches,' the giant striker joked afterwards. 'The bookmakers made us favourites to go down at the start of the season – we had a good laugh about that. I am sure we can keep our good form going as with our style of play we are always likely to score goals.'

28th September 1996

A 2-0 victory at Derby County, the Dons' fifth league win in a row, saw Joe Kinnear's side go third in the early Premier League table. Playing a classic counter-attacking game, the visitors absorbed all the Rams' first-half pressure before hitting them twice on the break after the interval. 'There are lots of good things happening at the moment,' the manager enthused. 'We're very sharp and very quick and scoring goals for fun.'

29th September 2001

Two goals each from strikers David Connolly and Neil Shipperley saw Kevin Keegan's expensively assembled Manchester City team put to the sword. 'This goes close to being the best result since I took over,' manager Terry Burton commented after his side's 4-0 First Division win at Maine Road. 'We have had an awful time with injuries but if that team keeps playing in the same way, then it will be difficult for players to get back in even when they are fit.'

29th September 2009

An early goal from Ross Montague was enough for the Dons to beat Rushden & Diamonds and move up to fourth in the Blue Square Premier table. 'We are a very young side and the aim this year was to gradually progress and make our move later in the campaign,' manager Terry Brown said. 'The last thing I want is for the team to think we are the finished article. There is still a lot of work to do, and it is my job to ensure that the players know it.'

30th September 1964

Before a midweek crowd of 5,123, the Dons beat table-topping Hereford United 2-1 to end the hosts' unbeaten Southern League Division One record at Edgar Street. Full-back Brian Rudge handed the Bulls an unfortunate lead in the 13th minute when he put the ball into his own net, but Eddie Reynolds soon restored parity. Just before the hour, Mickey Moore put Wimbledon ahead and the visitors held on to record a notable victory.

30th September 2013

The club revealed it was working with Galliard Homes to build a new community-focused stadium on the greyhound site on Plough Lane. 'There is a long way to go before the plans become a reality,' chief executive Erik Samuelson said. 'First, we need the support of Merton Council for a football stadium on the site. Second the designation must be reviewed and accepted by an independent adjudicator. The long-term aim is to get us back to our spiritual home.'

AFC
WIMBLEDON
On This Day

OCTOBER

1st October 1988

Having just signed for £125,000 from Nottingham Forest, Hans Segers enjoyed the sort of debut that would not have looked out of place in *Roy of the Rovers*. Having set up John Fashanu's opening goal with a long kick down the field he produced two late saves to deny a powerful Everton side as the Dons held out for a 2-1 win, their first of the season. 'People have been having digs at us so it was nice to show what we could do,' manager Bobby Gould said.

1st October 1997

Using several squad players for a midweek League Cup trip to lower-league Millwall, the Dons emerged from the New Den with an impressive 9-2 aggregate win. Wimbledon scored four but could easily have doubled their tally had their forwards have not been so wasteful in front of goal. 'The lads who came in did superbly for me,' manager Joe Kinnear enthused. 'It was an excellent performance. It was a young team, and it shows the potential we have at the club.'

2nd October 1991

The lowest top-flight attendance since the war, just 3,121, watched as goals from Dean Blackwell and Aidan Newhouse helped the Dons see off a spirited Sheffield Wednesday side 2-1 at Selhurst Park. It meant that when departing manager Ray Harford was replaced by Peter Withe following a victory over Norwich City the next Saturday, Wimbledon were sitting pretty in sixth place.

2nd October 1999

Alarm bells started ringing about the Dons' defensive frailties after bottom-of-the-table Sheffield Wednesday secured their first Premier League win of the season. Despite taking the lead through John Hartson, Wimbledon surrendered tamely at Hillsborough as they lost 5-1. 'After the game, the players were in a combination of shock, disbelief, and disappointment,' assistant coach Lars Tjærnås said. 'I have heard the word crisis mentioned, but that is something you associate with poverty in eastern Europe.'

3rd October 1960

Nearly 9,000 fans turned out at Plough Lane to see the club turn on its first set of floodlights prior to a London Challenge Cup match against Arsenal's reserves. With future Wimbledon boss Mike Everitt starring in the visitors' midfield, the Gunners lit up the evening with a hat-trick from Peter Kane leading to a 4-1 win.

3rd October 1992

A wonder strike from Dalian Atkinson settled an exciting Premier League contest in Aston Villa's favour. The Dons had levelled at 2-2 when the burly forward picked up the ball in his own half before beating three men and chipping Hans Segers to produce the most exquisite of finishes. The 6,849 fans at a rain-soaked Selhurst Park had seen what *Match of the Day* viewers later voted as the show's goal of the season.

4th October 1983

Serving notice of their intention to emerge as a force in the football world, the Dons beat Brian Clough's Nottingham Forest 2-0 in a League Cup tie at Plough Lane. 'We will have to put up the sort of show Wimbledon put up tonight in the second leg or we will be out,' the Forest boss warned later. 'We should have lost the game by five and if I had a two-goal advantage I would be prepared to take on Real Madrid or a World XI. We were out-run and out-fought.'

4th October 2008

Trailing 2-0 and effectively out of the Conference South contest at Worcester City inside the first quarter, the Dons salvaged some pride by pulling two goals back in the second half. 'I am very disappointed with the result,' said manager Terry Brown at the end. 'The first 25 minutes was a catalogue of disasters caused by individual errors and, as a result, we left ourselves with a mountain to climb.'

5th October 1985

The Dons claimed the notable scalp of Norwich City as their Second Division promotion campaign started to gather pace. The 2-1 victory over the eventual champions at Carrow Road led home boss Ken Brown to say, 'Our game is playing it along the deck but [Lawrie] Sanchez and [Steve] Galliers would not let us – they were like terriers out there.'

5th October 2010

Danny Kedwell was on target as the Dons won 5-2 at fellow Blue Square Premier promotion hopefuls Mansfield Town. 'It was one of those nights where everything we tried just seemed to come off and, as a manager, you just sit back and enjoy it,' Terry Brown said. 'We are certainly not thinking about the title though. We've been poor on two occasions this season and lost both times. Championship-winning sides win even when they are playing badly.'

6th October 1984

An ugly off-the-ball incident between John Gayle and Vinnie Jones took the headlines away from the Dons' impressive win at Sheffield United. Afterwards, it was reported that United boss Dave Bassett had to step in when the two players attempted to re-enact their contretemps in the tunnel after the game. 'Vinnie, Gayley, conduct yourselves properly. You're professional footballers so act your age!' the former Dons boss was quoted as telling the pair.

6th October 2012

Rashid Yussuff's 90th-minute winner secured the Dons a 2-1 at Plymouth in what proved to be Simon Bassey's last game in caretaker charge. 'The boys kept going and deserved great credit for their performance today,' the interim manager said. 'Rashid is a class act who can do wonderful things with a football. Six points out of 12 is not a bad return and if I get the job permanently it would be fantastic. If I don't then I go out on a winning note knowing I have done my best.'

7th October 2006

Bogey side Hampton & Richmond Borough inflicted the Dons' first Ryman League Premier defeat of the season. 'Had we won we would have been second in the table, but we ran out of ideas, passion and commitment,' Dave Anderson reflected. In a move that was to have serious future consequences, the manager also revealed that former Wimbledon FC player Jermaine Darlington was now training with the squad.

7th October 2014

The Dons came from behind to beat Milton Keynes 3-2 in the EFL Paint Trophy. A goal from Adebayo Akinfenwa with nine minutes left set up a famous victory and led Neal Ardley to comment, 'I know what our fans have been through, and I know the pain that they've had, and I think this time we have beaten them fair and square.'

8th October 1988

Beginning to find their form after the post-FA Cup victory turmoil at the club, the Dons made it three wins in a row as they gained a hard-fought win at Villa Park. Manager Bobby Gould picked out 22-year-old goalscorer John Scales for special praise. 'The young man had an exceptional game,' he said. 'After a difficult introduction to First Division life last year he has learned his trade. He and Eric Young have been superb at the heart of the defence this season.'

8th October 2011

Goals from Jack Midson and Christian Jolley saw the Dons win at Morecambe to leapfrog their hosts and go third in the League Two table. 'We're pinching ourselves at the moment and feeling a bit giddy,' manager Terry Brown said as he contemplated his side's excellent start to life in the Football League. 'It was a really exhilarating performance, but I am taking nothing for granted – I believe we are now 16 points above the relegation zone.'

9th October 1982

Teenage stars Glyn Hodges and Kevin Gage each scored twice as the Dons ran in six goals and overwhelmed visiting Aldershot. Bassett's boys brushed aside the shock of falling behind to Dale Banton's early strike to record one of the biggest wins in the club's short Football League career. It left Wimbledon looking down on the rest of the Fourth Division from the top of the table.

9th October 2010

The Dons reduced the gap on Blue Square Premier leaders Crawley Town to just one point after riding their luck to win at Wrexham. Outplayed for much of the game, second-half goals from Christian Jolley and Rashid Yussuff eventually produced a 2-1 win in north Wales. 'A spirited second-half performance saw us come away with an unlikely three points,' a relieved Terry Brown commented.

10th October 2009

Lewis Taylor scored one and set up two more as the Dons' positive start to their first season of Blue Square Premier football continued with a 5-2 win at Forest Green Rovers. 'We came down here expecting a very tight affair, but this was nothing of the sort,' Terry Brown said. 'It was an open, expansive game by both sides, who produced great attacking play, and, at times, abysmal defending.'

10th October 2016

The Dons celebrated the fourth anniversary of Neal Ardley's appointment as manager by winning at Oxford to move ahead of Milton Keynes in the football pyramid for the first time. 'That first season when I took the job was so difficult and at that point you think if I do not keep us up that could be me in management,' Ardley said. 'That was pivotal. So, to have four years and achieve what we have, I am really proud of it.'

11th October 2005

Dominating Ryman League leaders Hampton and Richmond Borough for long periods, the Dons' visit to the Beveree ultimately ended in a 2-1 defeat. 'Our luck has been so bad we are trying to find out which player has run over a black cat so we can put him on the transfer list,' manager Dave Anderson quipped wryly.

11th October 2012

Describing his appointment as 'like coming home', 40-year-old Neal Ardley warned against expectations that he would recreate the Crazy Gang at a press conference on the day after he became manager of AFC Wimbledon. 'Football has changed since I played for the club,' he said. 'You've got to be careful trying to recreate something when the game's moved on so much in 15 to 20 years. The one thing we'll try to do is create our own team spirit and environment we believe in.'

12th October 1996

Neil Sullivan pulled off two astonishing late saves from Sheffield Wednesday's Andy Booth and David Hirst to allow the Dons to stretch their winning Premier League run to six. With his side leading 3-2, the goalkeeper's contribution proved crucial before Vinnie Jones nodded home in the 86th minute to complete a 4-2 victory that moved Wimbledon up to fifth place ahead of a trip to Chelsea the following weekend.

12th October 2013

Any frustration that Wimbledon fans felt after it took a late Alan Bennett header for their team to secure a League Two point against rock-bottom Accrington were cast aside by the news that the club had submitted a detailed planning proposal for a move back to Plough Lane. 'It could complete the circle of a romantic story,' chief executive Erik Samuelson said. 'There is a long way to go before our dream becomes a reality, but this is an important step along the road.'

13th October 1993

Without a weekend Premier League match, the Dons faced Real Madrid in a four-team tournament in Santander. 'We went 2-0 down to goals from [Rafael Martín] Vázquez and [Emilio] Butragueño but showed great guts to pull ourselves back to 2-2 with goals from Alan Kimble and Dean Holdsworth,' manager Joe Kinnear said. 'Then Míchel let fly with a 35-yarder with two minutes to go. I hope the trip acts as a dress rehearsal and that next year we will be back to take on Real Madrid in a real competition.'

13th October 2012

Neal Ardley took charge of his first game, a 2-1 home defeat to Cheltenham Town. 'It was a strange day for me,' the new manager said. 'It didn't feel like my team. I was on the bench in name and body only. It was hard to talk about specifics because I did not know the players well enough. It was emotional, it was enjoyable, but it was horrible to lose. The supporters were great, but we have got to look like we are progressing and get results because it will soon stop being romantic.'

14th October 1978

The Dons increased their lead at the top of the Fourth Division table by stretching their unbeaten league run to 12 games following a 3-1 win over Scunthorpe United at Plough Lane. With his injury list growing, manager Dario Gradi announced that he would be looking to strengthen his squad. 'I have youngsters like Mick Sorenson and Wally Downes in the reserves but if we have further injuries we are going to be in trouble,' he said.

14th October 2000

A thrilling First Division match ebbed and flowed until Carl Asaba's late goal for Gillingham ensured a 4-4 draw. The Dons' injury-hit defence looked vulnerable in the air and the hosts found themselves trailing 3-2 at the break only for Jason Euell and John Hartson to put them ahead soon afterwards. 'I've scored eight goals in eight games since my move to Rangers fell through,' the Welsh striker said. 'Hopefully, we can now move up the table.'

15th October 1977

Showing signs of settling into their new surroundings, the Dons recorded their first away victory in the Football League, at AFC Bournemouth. 'We should have won more comfortably,' claimed manager Allen Batsford, 'and we would have done if our finishing had been sharper. But it is great to win away at last. It should help us to relax and believe in ourselves.' Goals either side of half-time from Billy Holmes and John Leslie put the visitors in control before the Cherries' late consolation.

15th October 2011

The Dons' bright start to life as a League Two club came to an end when they lost 3-1 to Crewe Alexandra at Kingsmeadow. Having played brilliantly without reward in the first period, fifth-placed Wimbledon were undone as Dario Gradi's team took them apart after the break. It was to be the new year before Terry Brown's boys recorded another league victory.

16th October 1999

Rumoured to be on a £10,000 bonus for every goal he scored, man of the match John Hartson grabbed a brace to help the Dons to their first Premier League win since the opening day of the season. 'I couldn't believe what I was watching,' Bradford City boss Paul Jewell commented after seeing his side lose 3-2. 'We seemed to be just there to make up the numbers.'

16th October 2007

Terry Brown did not mince his words after the Dons had crashed out of the FA Cup – beaten on penalties after extra time at Horsham. 'This side as an attacking force is not good enough and I will be making changes,' he said. 'This is one of the big nights at Horsham,' home boss John Maggs said. 'It is the first time we've beaten them. I think we just about deserved it.'

17th October 2009

The realities of life in the Blue Square Premier were only too apparent as Kettering Town inflicted the Dons' second successive home defeat by winning 2-1 at Kingsmeadow. 'The team are finding it more difficult to obtain victories at home than away,' manager Terry Brown admitted. 'Kettering, like Kidderminster in our previous game here, shut down the space and gave our passing players little time on the ball. It is a wake-up call.'

17th October 2017

Lyle Taylor ended a 21-game goal drought by scoring a hat-trick in the 3-1 League One defeat of Rotherham United. 'It's a good feeling,' the striker said. 'It's nice after six and a half months to actually score a goal – let alone three! It's kind of poetic really. My first appearance for this club in a pre-season friendly [against Basingstoke Town] was a hat-trick and when we needed a performance and some goals it was my turn.'

18th October 1997

Rumours that the club would soon be relocating to the Republic of Ireland took the gloss off a 2-1 Premier League win at Villa Park secured thanks to a second-half strike from teenager Carl Cort. Co-owner Kjell Inge Røkke was quoted as saying, 'We wouldn't have invested all this money unless we had the chance to compete with Arsenal, Chelsea and Spurs with a comparable crowd and stadium in Dublin.'

18th October 2015

Jon Meades's stoppage-time goal secured a 2-1 League One win at Gigg Lane. 'It was a real test of character to come to a wet and windy Bury on a horrible Tuesday night and win the game,' manager Neal Ardley commented. 'We knew that not so many of our fans would be able to travel, even though the support we did have was phenomenal. Getting up to Manchester on a Tuesday night is murder! The boys went up to our fans at the end to say thank you.'

19th October 1996

The Dons moved level on points with Arsenal at the top of the Premier League after a win at Stamford Bridge. Defending deep and attacking with pace, the visitors caused Chelsea's multinational team problems all afternoon as goals from Robbie Earle, Neal Ardley, Marcus Gayle and Efan Ekoku led to a 4-2 victory. 'Our aim is to finish in the top eight and win a European place next season,' Kinnear told the press afterwards. 'Now people are starting to believe us.'

19th October 2019

Terell Thomas scored a dramatic late winner against Portsmouth as the Dons recorded their third victory under caretaker boss Glyn Hodges. The next day it was announced that the suspended Wally Downes had been sacked. Having admitted breaching football's betting regulations, the 58-year-old lost his job after it was confirmed that he had been fined and banned following an FA enquiry.

20th October 1984

One of the most bizarre goals ever seen at Plough Lane helped the Dons beat Second Division leaders Portsmouth 3-2. Alan Cork had just fired Wimbledon ahead and, when Pompey kicked off, their goalkeeper was still lying on the ground and nursing an injury. It meant that when centre-back Noel Blake attempted a back pass without looking, the ball went straight into the unguarded net. 'A minute's lunacy in 90 cost us,' was visiting boss Alan Ball's brief post-match comment.

20th October 2015

Having publicly questioned his future as manager after a 5-2 home defeat at the hands of Morecambe the previous Saturday, Neal Ardley was delighted when his team came from two goals down to win 4-3 at promotion-chasing Accrington. 'We deserved the win, from ten minutes on we battered them,' he said. By the time his side returned to the Crown Ground the following May, they had moved from being mid-table mediocrities to become play-off contenders.

21st October 1995

With Vinnie Jones taking over in goal for the final 35 minutes after Paul Heald had been dismissed, the injury-hit Dons lost 6-1 at Newcastle United. 'I don't know what else can go wrong,' manager Joe Kinnear said. 'The difference between us coming here this season and last is £20m. That is how much they have spent on their squad while I got a goalkeeper for £125,000 in the summer. It is very tough, but we want to stay in there, punching with the best in the Premier League.'

21st October 2008

Goals from Jon Main and Danny Kedwell saw pre-season favourites Havant & Waterlooville put to the sword at Kingsmeadow. The big-spending Hawks were second-best all over the pitch as Wimbledon returned to the top of the Conference South table. 'Danny and Mainey are the best pairing in this league and they both love scoring goals,' manager Terry Brown enthused. 'If they stay fit and in form we will be there or thereabouts in April.'

22nd October 2005

A resolute performance allowed the mid-table Dons to beat high-flying Fisher Athletic 1-0 in a Ryman Premier League clash at Kingsmeadow. 'At last, we seem to be getting the results our performances deserve,' manager Dave Anderson said. 'They are my favourites for the title so I knew that we would have to be at our best today and our game plan worked very well. I thought we were well worth the win.'

22nd October 2016

Unbeaten in eight league matches, the Dons climbed into the League One play-off places courtesy of a 1-0 success at Peterborough United. The only goal arrived during a first half of Wimbledon dominance when Tom Elliott nodded in after Jon Meades had headed a tenth-minute George Francomb corner back across goal. 'It was the most one-sided game I've ever been involved in,' manager Neal Ardley said. 'We had so many chances and they could not get out of their half.'

23rd October 1999

Only the brilliance of Neil Sullivan allowed the Dons to hold on for a point at Villa Park after Dion Dublin equalised Robbie Earle's effort. The goalkeeper made three outstanding stops as Aston Villa pushed for a winner in a one-sided second half. 'Sully is in top form right now,' manager Egil Olsen said. 'I don't think that there are many better goalkeepers in the Premiership. Today the result was far better than the performance; maybe we were lucky for once.'

23rd October 2010

A 71st-minute goal from centre-back Ed Harris was enough to allow the Dons to progress to the first round of the FA Cup at the expense of Basingstoke Town. But the Blue Square Premier leaders were not at their best against spirited opposition and Seb Brown had to make several superb saves. 'The result was more important than the performance,' manager Terry Brown said. 'This is a very difficult place to win, and I am happy to have avoided a potential banana skin.'

24th October 1998

Thunder and lightning engulfed Selhurst Park as Wimbledon were denied what would have been a deserved victory over high-flying Middlesbrough. Lightning came from the heavens and the thunder from Joe Kinnear as he launched an attack on one of the linesmen following a 2-2 draw. '[Hamilton] Ricard was yards offside,' the manager fumed about Boro's second goal. 'Television said [Marcus] Gayle's late header was over the line – it is hard to take.'

24th October 2012

The Dons eased past Bristol Rovers to give manager Neal Ardley his first win in charge. Goals from Rashid Yussuff, Will Antwi and an own goal gave Wimbledon a 3-1 win. 'It was a dreadful first half,' Rovers boss Mark McGhee said after what proved to be his last match in charge. 'When we lost the first goal, we lost our shape and our energy.'

25th October 1997

Michael Hughes was branded a 'cheat' by Leeds boss George Graham after falling over the leg of David Hopkin to gain the first-half penalty that gave the Dons a 1-0 Premier League victory at Selhurst Park. Hopkin almost made amends after Neal Ardley had fired Wimbledon in front from the spot by hitting a post before the break but afterwards the hosts restricted the Yorkshire side to very few openings as they held on to record their second home win of the season.

25th October 2003

Paul Scott scored the third goal as the Dons beat leaders Chipstead 3-0 to move back to the top of the Combined Counties League. 'It was an excellent result against a good side,' manager Terry Eames said. 'I was pleased with the attitude of the players; they gave their all. Danny Oakins and Matt Everard were immense at the back; they didn't let anything get past them in the air or on the ground. They shouldn't be playing at this level.'

26th October 1965

Having won four away games in a row, a confident Dons side returned to Plough Lane to beat high-flying Cambridge United and go fourth in the Southern League Premier Division table. Playing in their first year at the top of the non-league game, a midweek crowd of 2,856 watched goals either side of half-time from Les Brown and Ian Cooke give the hosts another victory.

26th October 2002

Kevin Cooper was one of the scorers as the Dons beat Cobham 4-0 at Kingsmeadow to record their seventh successive Combined Counties League win. Commercial manager Ivor Heller was excited but realistic after hearing the news that Safeway was putting the site of the club's old stadium up for sale. 'It would be a dream to move back to Plough Lane and we will do everything we can to achieve that, but £12m is a lot of money,' he said.

27th October 1993

The Dons took advantage of striker Andy Cole's absence to move into the last 16 of the League Cup by beating Newcastle United 2-1 at Selhurst Park. With Wimbledon due on Tyneside the following weekend, Joe Kinnear feared a backlash from the Magpies. 'We've said all along that the cups are our main target this season and we're very glad to have got through this match,' the manager stated. 'The problem is we might have just wound them up for Saturday.'

27th October 2018

Time was nearly up for Neal Ardley as the Dons' dismal League One form continued with a 2-0 home defeat at the hands of Luton Town. 'I am under no illusions about what will happen if we don't turn our form around very soon,' the manager said in the week that followed. His six-year managerial reign came to an end two games later following a laboured FA Cup victory at a rain-swept Haringey Borough.

28th October 1995

Beating Southampton's Dave Beasant with a brilliant 20-yard shot on the turn in the 64th minute, 18-year-old Jason Euell's debut goal was the one bright spot of another Premier League defeat. 'You have to take a positive view of things and at least I will be driving home happy knowing we have unearthed a gem in Jason,' Kinnear said, despite the fact that future Don Neil Shipperley had scored in each half to secure the visitors a 2-1 win.

28th October 2006

Backed by more than 1,500 fans, the Ryman League Dons bowed out of the FA Cup after losing at Conference National pace-setters Exeter City. 'It was a strange experience watching yourself on *Football Focus* on Saturday morning and then be back doing the day job delivering wine on Monday,' manager Dave Anderson said as he reflected on the events of that weekend. 'Our support was incredible. It was emotional – that I can tell you.'

29th October 2005

The Dons returned to form with a 4-0 Ryman Premier League win at Windsor and Eton. 'I had asked the players for a reaction following the Bromley defeat and I think I got the perfect response,' manager Dave Anderson commented after his side had moved up into the top five. 'To be 3-0 up at half-time in a league match is always pleasing and we tried to go out and win the second half as well.'

29th October 2011

After conceding 12 goals in their three previous League Two matches, a 0-0 draw at Shrewsbury Town was just what the doctor ordered for the Dons. With Terry Brown again absent as he cared for his sick wife, his assistant Stuart Cash sounded satisfied. 'I spoke to Terry just after the game and he was happy with a point,' he said. 'After all the goals we have been conceding recently we changed our formation, and the object was to come here and get a clean sheet.'

30th October 1993

The Dons beat Swindon Town 3-0 to move into the top half of the Premier League table. 'We have the Crazy Gang image, and it creates camaraderie,' chief executive David Barnard said as he tried to explain the club's continuing success in an era of spiralling wages. 'Our owner, Sam Hammam, is a family man and he creates a family atmosphere. He knows all the schoolboy players by name and attends all the youth games – you cannot say that about many clubs.'

30th October 1994

Efan Ekoku's first goal for the Dons, against his old club Norwich City, secured a narrow and much-needed Premier League win. The Nigerian international latched on to a mistake for a 62nd-minute winner. 'Our game plan was to keep it tight at the back, not let in any goals and try to nick one,' a relieved Joe Kinnear said. 'After a bad run we showed today that we are getting back to some good habits.'

30th October 2004

The biggest non-league crowd of the day – 3,268 – witnessed the renewal of a fierce rivalry that had last been played 40 years before as the Dons came from behind twice to salvage a barely deserved Ryman League First Division draw against Tooting & Mitcham United. 'I thought we were awful in the first half, but we sorted it out at half-time,' reckoned manager Dave Anderson. 'In the last 30 minutes we played really well.'

31st October 1987

Goals from John Fashanu, Terry Gibson and John Gannon secured the Dons a 3-0 win over Spurs at White Hart Lane. With the national press heaping unexpected praise on the visitors, manager Bobby Gould paid fulsome tribute to the work of his number two, Don Howe, in changing the team's style of play. 'We are trying to make ourselves as difficult to beat as possible,' he added, 'but it is great when we score three goals away from home.'

31st October 1992

Lawrie Sanchez was in the right place at the right time to poach an 80th-minute winner at Old Trafford and blow a hole in Manchester United's aspiration to be the first winners of the Premier League. It was no more than the visitors deserved as Dean Holdsworth saw a first-half effort brilliantly blocked by Peter Schmeichel. It left Joe Kinnear commenting, 'We're changing, evolving and when we get it right, I think we'll be a quality team.'

AFC WIMBLEDON

On This Day

NOVEMBER

1st November 1983

Taking the plaudits, having opened the scoring before supplying two perfect in-swinging corners for Alan Cork to add two more, Glyn Hodges made clear his team were serious Third Division promotion contenders after beating Oxford United 3-1. 'Jim Smith's side will be up the top come May and I thought we were excellent and well worth our win,' the 20-year-old said. 'I thought we battered them and eventually they submitted.'

1st November 1986

Quickly dubbed 'The Battle of White-Hot Lane' by the tabloids, red cards for Graham Roberts and Lawrie Sanchez overshadowed the Dons' 2-1 win at Tottenham Hotspur in their first year in the top flight. 'When we lose, we are accused of being boring and when we win, we are a load of thugs,' manager Dave Bassett told the press pack. 'I am used to the criticism now. No one likes it but I let the comments roll off my back.'

2nd November 1889

A team of former pupils from the Central School in Wimbledon took to the field for a home game for the first time. The forerunners of the modern club made their historic debut on Wimbledon Common, playing on a pitch near Robin Hood Road after changing in a local pub. In its match report, the local paper declared the 1-0 win over Westminster 'an exciting game'.

2nd November 1996

The Dons had to settle for a point at the end of what manager Joe Kinnear called 'a blinding match' – a top-of-the-table Premier League clash with Arsenal played in front of 25,521 fans at Selhurst Park. Twice behind, the Dons levelled thanks to goals from Vinnie Jones and Marcus Gayle. Despite both sides creating late openings, the score remained 2-2 at the close.

2nd November 2013

The lights went out on League Two highfliers Rochdale as the Dons came from behind to win 2-1 at Spotland. The scores were level at 1-1 with quarter of an hour to go when play was halted for 25 minutes after lightning struck one of the floodlights and plunged the ground into darkness. But when the match restarted, Andy Frampton took advantage of a weaving run and pass from Kevin Sainte-Luce to lash home what proved to be the winner.

3rd November 1962

Some 9,500 fans inside Plough Lane saw the Isthmian League Dons knock Third Division Colchester United out of the FA Cup. Goals from Les Brown and Eddie Reynolds either side of half-time had put the hosts in control before the Us scored with ten minutes left. 'They were the better side on the day and took their few chances in grand style,' a magnanimous Colchester boss Ted Fenton said after Wimbledon held out for a famous victory.

3rd November 2007

'We are ten points behind them in the league and if you had given me the choice on Saturday morning between the win and the ten points, I would have taken the points,' manager Terry Brown admitted after his Dons side had beaten runaway Ryman League leaders Chelmsford City 4-0 in the FA Trophy. With just one automatic promotion spot available, Wimbledon never did manage to catch the Clarets and had to go up via the play-offs.

3rd November 2020

Doncaster Rovers denied the Dons a winning start on their return to their spiritual home at Plough Lane after a 29-year absence, coming from behind twice to earn a dramatic 2-2 draw in a match played behind closed doors due to Covid rules. 'It's great to be back,' manager Glyn Hodges said. 'I know there's going to be another homecoming with the fans here. That's going to be a great party.'

4th November 1984

Three goals in five second-half minutes helped the Dons to beat Crystal Palace in the first league meeting between the sides. With the Dons behind to Peter Nicholas's early penalty, the Second Division fixture came alive when they turned the game on its head through goals from Andy Sayer, Nigel Winterburn and Alan Cork. Although the Eagles pulled one back before the end, it was a day of celebration for the home fans in the 7,674 crowd.

4th November 1987

Quoted before the game as saying, 'My rag, tag and bobtail outfit has no chance against the Liverpool Rolls-Royce,' manager Bobby Gould claimed afterwards that a 1-1 draw against the unbeaten First Division leaders was a fair result. The hosts had refused to be overawed against the men from Anfield and used the lessons learned to stop the Reds gaining a league and cup double at Wembley the following May.

5th November 2002

With Bonfire Night fireworks exploding all around them, the Dons rocketed up into second place in the Combined Counties League table after a convincing win at Cove. After taking a two-goal lead in the first quarter of the match, the visitors scored twice more early in the second period and looked as though they would cartwheel to a big victory but, instead, they fired blanks during a dull final half an hour.

5th November 2011

The Dons had to come from behind to secure a 1-1 League Two draw with Lawrie Sanchez's Barnet at Kingsmeadow. With Wimbledon boss Terry Brown absent on compassionate leave following his wife's cancer operation, the struggling Bees deserved their point. 'We are all missing Terry,' assistant manager Stuart Cash said. 'He is a focal point for this football club and has been a major driving force to getting us to this level.'

6th November 1995

Having just returned to the touchline after completing a six-month ban, Joe Kinnear risked further FA retribution by calling referee Paul Alcock a 'disgrace' after the official had sent off Vinnie Jones in a 4-1 defeat at Nottingham Forest. On the back of a 25-match unbeaten league run, the hosts were far too strong for a woeful Wimbledon side that slipped to fourth bottom of the table after their seventh successive Premier League defeat.

6th November 2004

Three second-half goals settled the battle of the Dons in favour of north London as Ryman League First Division AFC Wimbledon were well-beaten at Premier League Hendon in an FA Trophy first-round tie. 'I know it ruins the fans' weekend when we lose but I can assure you that no one had a worse night than me after that,' manager Dave Anderson reflected after his return to Claremont Road had been spoiled.

7th November 1998

Taking advantage of the obvious discord in the Nottingham Forest camp, the Dons recorded an away Premier League victory at the City Ground courtesy of Marcus Gayle's first-half header. 'My old Wimbledon team would have taken him into a corner and given him a good hiding,' home goalkeeper Dave Beasant said of his colleague, Pierre van Hooijdonk, who had just returned to the team following a one-man strike.

7th November 1999

A goal in each half was enough for the Dons to down Premier League leaders Leeds United at Selhurst Park. Less than fresh after their Champions League match in Moscow the previous Thursday night, the weary visitors were taken apart as Wimbledon secured just their third victory of the campaign. 'John Hartson was immense,' manager Egil Olsen said afterwards. 'This win is important, and I am very pleased with the clean sheet, but there is still a long way to go.'

8th November 1958

Twenty-one-year-old Croydon-based plumber Roy Law kept the dangerous Paddy Hasty largely at bay in a drawn Isthmian League derby against Tooting & Mitcham United. When the Irishman did escape the centre-half's clutches moments before half-time, he fired the Terrors in front, and it took a well-taken 66th-minute equaliser from skipper Jim Wright to ensure the blue half of the 6,946 crowd went home reasonably happy.

8th November 2005

Goals from Richard Butler and Sonny Farr were enough to remove a powerful Staines side from the Ryman League Cup on a freezing night in west London. There was sad news when it was announced that former favourite Matt Everard had retired from the game due to recurring knee trouble. 'I had hoped to return to playing,' he said, 'but the doctors have told me to stop so I have to follow their advice.'

9th November 1994

Norwegian international Øyvind Leonhardsen made a goalscoring debut as the Dons beat Aston Villa 4-3 in a thrilling Premier League match at Selhurst Park. The visitors were 2-1 up when Andy Townsend was ordered off and despite falling further behind Wimbledon turned it round with second-half strikes from Neal Ardley, Vinnie Jones and, in the last minute, Leo himself. After a run of eight defeats in nine games, Villa boss Ron Atkinson was sacked the following morning.

9th November 2002

A record crowd at Merstham of 1,587 saw the Dons record their 13th successive league and cup victory and move just three points behind unbeaten Combined Counties League leaders AFC Wallingford. 'It has all been brilliant,' Merstham chairman Ted Hickman said afterwards. 'The Dons fans have been superb. I walked around the pitch and shook hands with as many of them as possible. It was the biggest thing that had ever happened in the history of Merstham FC.'

10th November 2007

A single-goal victory over AFC Hornchurch eased the Dons into the Ryman Premier League play-off places. Tony Finn continued his hot streak with an early goal and despite Luke Garrard having to replace the injured Andy Little in goal at half-time, the visitors rarely threatened. 'Luke showed not only his dedication to the club but also his love of the game with a typically brave and eccentric performance,' manager Terry Brown said.

10th November 2008

Sam Hatton scored a consolation goal as the Dons were knocked out of the FA Cup in a televised Kingsmeadow clash, beaten 4-1 by League Two Wycombe Wanderers. 'When you play against a team from a higher league you need to make them work hard for their goals and we clearly didn't do that tonight,' a disappointed Terry Brown said afterwards.

11th November 1975

A wonderful night of football culminated in Billy Holmes grabbing the vital extra-time goal that brought the Non-League Championship Challenge trophy to Plough Lane for the first time. Having lost the first leg 1-0 to Northern Premier League title holders Wigan, the reigning Southern League champions took until the hour to level through Ian Cooke and there were less than 15 minutes of extra time remaining when the former Barnet striker struck the winner.

11th November 1989

Vaughan Ryan emerged as an unlikely hero as the Dons beat Tottenham Hotspur 1-0 at White Hart Lane. 'I didn't expect to play but the boss asked me to do a man-to-man marking job on dangerman Paul Gascoigne and I just went out there and did it,' the young midfielder was quoted as saying. 'I dived in a couple of times early on but once I had got my composure I was pleased with my performance.'

12th November 2012

Extra-time goals from Byron Harrison and Jack Midson saw the Dons beat York City 4-3 in a pulsating FA Cup replay to set up a first meeting with Milton Keynes. 'I have been following Wimbledon since 1982, at nine I was a mascot against Hull City in the old Fourth Division, but here I was, half-praying for defeat,' supporter Niall Couper commented as a fixture against Franchise loomed.

12th November 2017

A series of theatrical dives did nothing to endear Peterborough's Marcus Maddison to the crowd as the Dons came from behind to claim a 2-2 draw in a televised League One clash at Kingsmeadow. Manager Neal Ardley sounded satisfied despite the fact that his side remained in the bottom four, 'Overall, in the end, in an end-to-end game we might have nicked it, but we might have lost it. We have to take the point and the performance as a positive one,' he said.

13th November 1965

Twenty-year-old Ian Cooke was the Wimbledon hero as his hat-trick helped to defeat Gravesend 4-1 in the FA Cup first round at Plough Lane. Having threatened to forfeit the tie by leaving the field for several minutes in protest following full-back Pat Brady's first-half dismissal, the visitors were made to pay on their return. 'The referee made an appalling decision when he sent him off,' 'Fleet manager Walter Ricketts claimed afterwards, 'but I could not allow them to walk off.'

13th November 2004

The name of AFC Wimbledon went into the history books after Rob Ursell's strike at Bromley secured a draw and stretched the club's unbeaten record to 76 games. 'We started out having trials on Wimbledon Common with players of all shapes and sizes,' the club's first captain, Joe Sheerin, commented. 'I never imagined I would be part of something like this. No matter who's come and gone, we've maintained consistency. That's special.'

14th November 1975

The Dons extended their winning run to 20 matches by beating World Cup-winning right-back George Cohen's Tonbridge Angels 4-0 at Plough Lane. But with almost half of their fixtures so far being cup ties, they were still four points behind Southern League leaders Yeovil Town, albeit with six games in hand. The winning run was to continue for two more matches before Allen Batsford's side drew 1-1 at Cambridge City in the first game in December.

14th November 2009

With James Pullen and Danny Kedwell not fit enough to make the long journey to the Furness peninsula, the Dons did well to fight back from two goals down to secure a draw at Barrow. All looked lost after an hour's play in Cumbria but goals from Jon Main and Elliott Godfrey plus a full-length save from young Seb Brown in the last minute ensured the visitors travelled home with a point.

15th November 2008

Making their first visit to Park View Road since their Wimbledon predecessors had beaten a Bexleyheath & Welling side there in 1962, the Dons twice took the lead in a Conference South clash with Welling United before being forced to settle for a draw. Jon Main fired the visitors ahead in the second minute only for Charlie Sheringham to bundle home an equaliser. A rare goal from Ben Judge immediately restored the lead but it was the future Don who again levelled things up.

15th November 2016

The Dons hit five in an FA Cup replay with Bury to set up a second-round meeting with Curzon Ashton. Dominic Poleon scored in each half and there were goals for Paul Robinson, Dean Parrett and Lyle Taylor as Wimbledon made their Lancashire opponents look very ordinary. 'The fans will have enjoyed tonight, but I would have taken 1-0 before the game,' Neal Ardley commented. 'They are a strong side, and I knew that they could hurt us if we let them.'

16th November 2013

An Andy Frampton brace set the Dons on their way to a 4-0 League Two victory over Portsmouth. Harry Pell had missed a penalty before the big centre-back headed the first of his two goals, and second-half strikes from Sammy Moore and Michael Smith completed a rout. It was a measure of how fast fortunes can change in football that five years earlier, as a part-time AFC Wimbledon outfit were enjoying their Conference South season, Premier League Pompey were winning the FA Cup.

16th November 2014

AFC Wimbledon submitted a planning application to Merton Council for a new stadium at Plough Lane. They proposed building an 11,000-capacity ground, which could be expanded to 20,000 later, on the site of Wimbledon Greyhound Stadium. 'This is the culmination of 18 months' intensive work,' chief executive Erik Samuelson said. 'It is an extremely comprehensive proposal covering every aspect of the development and associated issues.'

17th November 1969

Nearly 5,000 spectators saw Wimbledon lose the London Challenge Cup Final 2-1 to Arsenal's reserves at Plough Lane. The Gunners fielded future Double winners Frank McLintock, Charlie George and Pat Rice in their line-up, alongside a certain Bobby Gould, and it was the future Dons boss who did the damage by scoring in each half to ensure the trophy went to north London. 'I am disappointed but not downhearted,' manager Les Henley commented. 'I thought we played well.'

17th November 2007

Just signed from fellow Ryman Leaguers Tonbridge Angels, Jon Main was forced to play second fiddle as the Dons came from behind to win 3-1 at Hastings thanks to two goals from much-criticised frontman Daniel Webb. 'Wimbledon want to be a Football League club in five or six years, and I would like to help them along the way,' the new striker revealed. 'We are now in third place, and I think we have a good chance of going up this year.'

18th November 2000

After Nottingham Forest equalised with just moments remaining, the City Ground was silenced by Trond Andersen's late First Division winner. 'That's typical Wimbledon isn't it,' Forest keeper Dave Beasant said. 'We thought we had snatched a draw with our late goal but seconds later they come back and stick it in our net. Wimbledon are never dead – I know that better than anyone.'

18th November 2010

Two Sammy Moore goals, one deep in stoppage time at the end of the 90 minutes and the other in the last moments of extra time, saw the Dons break Ebbsfleet hearts and advance into the second round of the FA Cup. The visitors were 2-1 down from the 19th minute onwards and, despite dominating the second half, it looked as though Terry Brown's boys were going out. 'It was one of those games where no one really deserves to lose,' the manager said.

19th November 1994

The Dons continued their revival by overcoming a red card for Vinnie Jones and a missed penalty to knock Newcastle United off the top of the Premier League table. Leading 3-2 at the break, ten-man Wimbledon held on in a breathless second half. 'Once again people have been too quick to write us off,' a buoyant Joe Kinnear commented. 'That's nine points from a possible 12 so perhaps we're not so bad a team after all for a team that every year is even money to be relegated.'

19th November 2003

Three goals down after 30 minutes at Walton Casuals, a brilliant fightback saw the Dons progress into the third round of the Combined Counties League Cup. Having pulled two goals back by the hour only for the visitors to score again, continuous pressure in the final quarter saw the hosts level before Matt Everard scored the winner eight minutes into injury time to complete a remarkable evening of football.

20th November 1976

Dickie Guy made his 500th appearance between the posts as the Dons edged past Isthmian League Woking in an FA Cup first-round tie. A 72nd-minute winner from Roger Connell, scored when a replay at Kingfield was looking increasingly likely, settled the tie. 'I sometimes think I would not mind playing behind a defence that was not so good,' the largely unemployed home custodian joked at the end. 'I might get more to do!'

20th November 2001

After years when they had been Premier League high rollers, all the fury of the fans was unleashed as lowly Walsall's equaliser, two minutes from time, left the Dons firmly outside the First Division promotion places. 'It was another frustrating evening for us as we dominated possession but could not finish the job,' manager Terry Burton commented. 'People expect you to roll over the likes of Walsall, but they are a decent side.'

21st November 1987

In a match given extra spice when Wimbledon turned down the visitors' offer of £400,000 for goalkeeper Dave Beasant in the lead-up, the Dons completed their third successive victory over Manchester United with a 2-1 win at Plough Lane thanks to second-half goals from Carlton Fairweather and John Scales. 'You know what you are getting when you come down here,' was Alec Ferguson's terse post-match comment.

21st November 1998

Efan Ekoku's 77th-minute goal was enough for the Dons to beat Premier League champions Arsenal. The Gunners created the better chances, but Wimbledon took one that came their way in the second period and then hung on grimly as the visitors tried to restore parity. 'They were more determined than us,' Arsenal manager Arsène Wenger said. 'We have to be conscious that every game is a fight. We did not do enough offensively. We were too poor to win.'

22nd November 1952

Drawn at fellow Isthmian Leaguers and defending FA Amateur Cup holders Walthamstow Avenue in the FA Cup first round, strikes from future Surrey cricket captain Mickey Stewart and the prolific Harry Stannard saw the Dons lead by two goals after an hour at Green Pond Lane. With a crowd of over 6,000 urging them on, the hosts hit back to equalise and in the Plough Lane replay the following week the A's triumphed 3-0.

Newcomer Jon Main had to be patient early on in his Dons career, but eventually he would go on to help the club achieve their goal of reaching the Football League.

22nd November 1997

After late goals had given Manchester United a 5-2 Premier League victory at Selhurst Park, Sam Hammam came out to confront fans who had stayed behind at the final whistle to protest over plans to move the Dons to Dublin. For his part, manager Joe Kinnear was unhappy at reports saying that the club's new owners wanted to replace him with former Norway coach Egil Olsen. 'If that is their intention, why don't they just pay up my contract and let me go?' he asked.

23rd November 1974

Mick Mahon's brilliant late strike, from fully 40 yards, knocked fellow Southern Leaguers Bath City out of the FA Cup and extended the Dons' winning run to an incredible 21 games in all competitions. 'I thought it was a great game,' press secretary Alex Fuce commented after a pulsating battle watched by 5,425 fans. 'We pulverised them for a time, they came back briefly and then we got that winner. It was the goal of the season.'

23rd November 2002

A police helicopter and 30 officers were called to a normally quiet Oxfordshire backwater to restore order after trouble flared during the Dons' Combined Counties League game with AFC Wallingford. A group, unconnected with either team, started taunting the Dons supporters and by the time calm had been established AFC Wimbledon – who had Joe Sheerin sent off – found themselves on the wrong end of a 3-0 scoreline.

24th November 1973

Southern League Wimbledon's FA Cup hopes were ended amid disgraceful scenes of crowd violence at The Walks in King's Lynn. Hopeful of progressing against lower-league opposition, the Dons and their followers were forced to take cover as play was suspended for nine minutes when hooligans invaded the pitch. Soon afterwards, the Linnets scored the only goal of the game leaving manager Dick Graham to admit, 'We played badly and deserved to lose.'

24th November 1993

John Fashanu's aerial challenge, in which his left elbow shattered the eyeball of Spurs centre-back Gary Mabbutt, completely overshadowed a 1-1 draw at White Hart Lane. The row that ensued occupied the back pages for weeks and eventually led to the Wimbledon striker being called to appear before an FA Disciplinary Committee. 'No one likes to see a fellow professional injured, but I did not set out to hurt him. I always go for the ball,' Fash commented.

25th November 1978

Backed by four coaches of fans, Fourth Division Wimbledon played out a goalless draw at Southern League Gravesend & Northfleet to secure an FA Cup first-round replay. Post Office clerical officer Lee Smelt emerged as the home hero after he saved Steve Parsons's twice-taken first-half penalty. After winning the replay in extra time, the Dons edged out AFC Bournemouth before being beaten by First Division Southampton in round three.

25th November 2000

Striker John Hartson pledged his loyalty to the cause after his goal had helped the Dons win 2-1 at Norwich in a First Division encounter. 'I want to make it clear that I am totally happy here,' he said, after a move to Charlton Athletic had fallen through. 'But if the club keep trying to sell me because of the wage bill and the fee they can command then it's out of my hands. I have said all along that we can make the play-offs and I have set myself a 25-goal target.'

26th November 1966

In atrocious conditions at London Road, the Southern League Dons exited the FA Cup at the first-round stage, beaten 2-1 by Midland League Grantham Town. Full-back Brian Martin had a nightmare match: under no pressure he headed an own goal past Frank Smith and then his hesitation contributed to the Gingerbreadmen getting their second, decisive goal in the 56th minute. His substitution was greeted by jeers from the travelling fans.

26th November 1996

Marcus Gayle scored the only goal in the first half as the Dons reached the League Cup quarter-finals for only the second time after knocking out holders Aston Villa at Selhurst Park. Heroic defending in the last few minutes – Kenny Cunningham kicked Andy Townsend's goal-bound effort off the line and Neil Sullivan made a brilliant save from Julian Joachim – allowed the hosts to withstand a late Villa barrage.

27th November 1980

Fourth Division Wimbledon put seven goals past Athenian League Windsor & Eton in a one-sided FA Cup first-round tie at Plough Lane. Ahead 2-1 at the interval thanks to two headers from Mick Smith, the hosts ran riot after the break with Dave Hubbick scoring a 15-minute hat-trick and Tommy Cunningham and Alan Cork adding late goals to make the final score 7-2. 'We wore them down and wore them out,' manager Dario Gradi said. 'They were not used to coping with continual pressure.'

27th November 2010

League Two Stevenage taught the non-league Dons a harsh lesson as they comfortably won a televised FA Cup second-round tie at Kingsmeadow. 'The end of this year's cup run was disappointing – it always is when you go out of a competition as famous as this,' manager Terry Brown said. 'But we have to be straight with ourselves and I can honestly say that the best side won.'

28th November 1979

A game of spectacular goals and brilliant attacking football ended with the Dons advancing into the second round of the FA Cup after beating Gillingham 4-2. John Leslie's early far-post header was quickly cancelled out by Ken Price before Steve Parsons restored the hosts' advantage. Mark Dziadulewicz then scored the best of the bunch when he curled home a fine strike but there was still time for Leslie and Price to exchange more goals before the referee blew for time.

28th November 2015

Adebayo Akinfenwa earned a point with a late header as the Dons came from behind at ten-man Leyton Orient. 'Forget the sending-off,' Neal Ardley said. 'I think from about the 20th or 25th minute on it was us that was the better team. We started the second half brilliantly again on the front foot, it was all us and then the sending-off sometimes can make it harder because they just sat in at that point and we just had to keep going.'

29th November 1986

Vinnie Jones announced his arrival on the national stage by scoring the winner as the Dons faced Manchester United for the first time. Signed for £8,000 from Wealdstone, the former hod carrier scored with a header from Glyn Hodges's corner early in the second half and celebrated by jumping on to the fence in front of the West Bank. 'He played well but he mustn't let it go to his head,' Dave Bassett counselled afterwards.

29th November 2006

On a night of high drama, the Dons advanced to face Aldershot Town in the first round proper of the FA Trophy by beating Eastleigh on penalties. The visitors were just seconds from going out when Lewis Cook sent in a cross that substitute Scott Fitzgerald fired home and the same combination fashioned an identikit goal to put Wimbledon ahead in extra time. After Steve West levelled the scores with a minute remaining, two full-length saves made Andy Little the hero of the shoot-out.

30th November 1988

With the rumour mill suggesting that Newcastle United were preparing a £1.5m bid for John Fashanu, the Dons looked largely toothless up front as they drew a League Cup fourth-round tie with QPR at Loftus Road. The visiting defence did well to protect Hans Segers in the Wimbledon goal as Bobby Gould denied his captain wanted to leave. 'I have not received a transfer request either verbally or in writing from John Fashanu,' he said.

30th November 1996

The Dons stretched their unbeaten run to 17 games as a 1-0 victory over Nottingham Forest at Selhurst Park kept them rubbing shoulders with Arsenal, Liverpool and Newcastle at the top of the Premier League. 'We always get more points in the second half of the season,' Kinnear told the press. 'We always finish strongly. But to win something we will have to be lucky with injuries and suspensions as we have no money to go out and buy more players.'

AFC WIMBLEDON

On This Day

DECEMBER

1st December 1990

A 4-0 top-flight win at Carrow Road was good enough to earn the Dons the Barclays Performance of the Week award and caretaker boss Ray Harford a permanent contract. John Fashanu's strike after 26 seconds set the scene for an opening half an hour in which the visitors simply swept aside their stunned hosts with four unanswered goals. 'I thought we were magnificent,' former Fulham coach Harford commented afterwards. 'The only problem was at half-time – I didn't know what to say.'

1st December 1993

Robbie Earle's 84th-minute header earned the Dons a deserved draw in a League Cup fourth-round tie at Liverpool. 'I am dumbfounded. I cannot comprehend how we managed to produce a performance like that,' Reds boss Graeme Souness commented. 'We will need to produce a much better performance when we go down there.' Wimbledon went on to win the replay on penalties.

2nd December 1989

The Dons took advantage of some embarrassing home defending to record a 5-2 victory at Stamford Bridge that earned them the Barclays Team of the Week award. 'I did not know that the ball had got away from him until I heard someone scream at me to turn, then I couldn't believe it,' Alan Cork said after Dave Beasant's howler handed him the first goal on a plate. 'That was the sort of chance strikers dream of.'

2nd December 2012

The Dons were desperately unlucky to lose an FA Cup second-round tie 2-1 at Milton Keynes in a match that aroused heated emotions. 'I was six weeks into my first managerial job, and I had to deal with a press conference with guys from places like Australia and New Zealand saying this was the most unique game ever,' Neal Ardley recalled. 'I wanted the fans to know how much I cared but I did not want to say something that would incite an already difficult situation.'

3rd December 1960

In shocking conditions at Plough Lane, a rampant Dons side put nine unanswered goals past Athenian League Leyton. With driving rain keeping the attendance below 2,000, stand-in centre-forward Joe Wallis grabbed a hat-trick and both Brian Martin and Norman Williams bagged a pair as Wimbledon advanced to the second round of the London Senior Cup.

3rd December 1995

Without a league or cup win since early September, the Dons were desperately unlucky not to beat a Newcastle United side sitting five points clear at the top of the Premier League table. Trailing 3-2 at half-time, Mick Harford levelled in the second period before Marcus Gayle twice went close in the closing moments. 'When we get it right on the day we are as good as anyone,' manager Joe Kinnear told the press.

4th December 1999

Goals from Carl Cort, Robbie Earle, John Hartson, Jason Euell and Marcus Gayle saw the Dons beat bottom-of-the-table Watford 5-0. But the club's record Premier League victory failed to impress manager Egil Olsen. 'We were poor in the first half and overall, I think we were very, very lucky and could have lost,' he said.

4th December 2016

The Dons hit back from 3-0 down with just ten minutes remaining to claim one of the most remarkable FA Cup victories in their long history. An Adam Morgan hat-trick had seemingly put National League North strugglers Curzon Ashton through to round three only for Wimbledon to strike back with three goals in two minutes from Tom Elliott, Dominic Poleon and Tyrone Barnett, before Elliott grabbed the winner deep into injury time.

5th December 1981

Fielding a makeshift side due to suspensions, injury and flu, the bottom-of-the-table Dons went down 3-2 at home to Newport County in a Third Division match played at Plough Lane. 'I seem to have lost my sharpness at the moment,' 22-year-old goalkeeper Dave Beasant said afterwards. 'I don't know why. I seem to be being beaten by some amazing 35-yard shots and I let one through my hands again today.'

5th December 2009

Goals from Steven Gregory and Ricky Wellard were enough for the Dons to beat Gateshead 2-0 during the club's first season of Blue Square Premier football. 'We have achieved four clean sheets in a row and picked up 12 points in the process and now sit in sixth position,' manager Terry Brown commented. 'We know we are only halfway through the league fixtures but find ourselves in a good position.'

6th December 1986

Goals from John Fashanu, Carlton Fairweather, Alan Cork and Vinnie Jones made the Dons' first league trip to Chelsea an afternoon to remember. The visitors were already 2-0 up when Doug Rougvie's studs-up challenge on Dave Beasant led to a 21-man brawl and the dismissal of the fiery Scotsman. 'I was sorry to see him go off,' Fashanu commented. 'He is my kind of opponent, but I have definitely crossed him off my Christmas card list.'

6th December 2008

The Dons showed some signs of returning to form as they won 2-1 at Team Bath to move up to sixth in the Conference South table. 'That was a much-needed win,' manager Terry Brown commented. 'I thought our players adapted very well to the difficult conditions and thoroughly deserved the victory. A look at the league table tells you how important those three points are and over Christmas we need to deliver the goods and go on a run of back-to-back wins.'

7th December 1963

Nearly 8,500 fans witnessed a brilliant FA Cup second-round tie at Plough Lane in which the Isthmian League Dons twice came from behind to force a replay against Southern League Bath City. Les Brown and Eddie Reynolds were on target for the hosts and afterwards Romans manager Malcolm Allison told everyone who would listen that his side would easily win the replay. The man who came to be known as 'Big Mal' was on the money as Wimbledon lost 4-0 at Twerton Park.

7th December 1996

Two excellent strikes from Efan Ekoku and a side-footed finish from Dean Holdsworth stretched the Dons' unbeaten Premier League and cup record to 19 matches after a 3-1 victory at Sunderland. 'The only other time I've experienced a run like this was after visiting a curry house,' Vinnie Jones quipped. Meanwhile, manager Joe Kinnear commented about his third-placed side, 'Europe is our priority.'

8th December 2012

Stacy Long's late equaliser salvaged a point for the Dons against League Two relegation rivals Barnet. Jake Hyde had scored the opener for the bottom-placed Bees with a close-range header before the midfield man levelled from the edge of the area with six minutes left. 'I'm pleased we gave the fans a performance that at least showed we were prepared to scrap and battle,' manager Neal Ardley said afterwards.

8th December 2018

Substitute Andy Barcham rescued a point as Wally Downes's first home game in charge ended with the Dons drawing 1-1 with Rochdale. 'If we hadn't turned it around, I would have had to be working on teamwork and motivation,' the new boss said. 'But they've set the standard and shown how determined they are not to lose and how willing they are to do what I'm asking them to do. I'm not going to let them drop below that.'

9th December 1967

Producing what the reporter from the local *Boro News* called 'unquestionably their best performance since turning professional', the Dons overcame blizzard-like conditions to beat a powerful Romford side 3-0 in the FA Cup first round at Plough Lane. With Wimbledon ahead, the visitors appealed in vain for the referee to abandon the game as snow continued to fall in the second half.

9th December 2000

Seemingly liberated away from Selhurst Park, the brilliant Dons shattered second-placed Birmingham City's unbeaten home record with a 3-0 victory at St Andrew's, the third goal coming after the 68th-minute dismissal of John Hartson. 'If we could produce our away form at home, we would be shooting up the [First Division] table,' manager Terry Burton said after admitting he was under pressure from the club's owners to sell some players to reduce the wage bill.

10th December 1988

Still trying to rebuild in the wake of the departures following their FA Cup success in May, the Dons lost 2-1 at lowly Newcastle United. 'When I joined, Bobby Gould assured me that whatever I had read about tensions within the club everyone pulled together on the field,' defender Keith Curle was quoted as saying. 'I have been impressed with the spirit in the squad since I moved here, and our aim is to climb the table before we defend the FA Cup in the new year.'

10th December 1994

Øyvind Leonhardsen and Mick Harford were on target as the Dons beat Coventry City 2-0 in the Premier League. 'It is always nice to put one over on an old club,' veteran striker Harford admitted. 'I was aggrieved when they sold me in the summer. I'd been out for a year and when I finally got fit, they did not give me a chance. I am enjoying myself here. The club is superbly run and there is a magnificent spirit about the place.'

11th December 1993

Aston Villa boss Ron Atkinson admitted he was impressed with the quality in the Wimbledon team after seeing his side beaten 1-0 at Villa Park following a late goal from Dean Holdsworth. 'We rarely get any credit for the hard work we do week in and week out but hopefully everyone realised how well we played today,' manager Joe Kinnear commented. 'We enjoy coming to the big clubs and poking them in the eye.'

11th December 2004

The Dons came from behind at half-time to win a Ryman League First Division clash 4-1 at Ashford Town (Middx). Deservedly trailing at the break, the visitors were transformed after an interval 'chat' from the management team, and goals from Gary Prigent, Richard Butler and Martin Randall put them in control by the hour. 'We played very well in the second half, but we need to learn we cannot keep getting away with starting games like that,' Dave Anderson said.

12th December 1992

Two goals apiece from Neil Ardley and Dean Holdsworth gave Wimbledon a 5-2 Premier League victory over Oldham Athletic at Selhurst Park. 'Christmas comes early when you play Oldham. We were terrible, we defended like women,' the Latics' decidedly non-PC boss Joe Royle offered. The attendance of just 3,386 was not what the architects of the 'super league' had envisaged when they had launched a 'whole new ball game' just six months earlier.

12th December 2009

Terry Brown's plan of playing some of his Blue Square Premier squad players against a solid but hardly inspiring Ryman League Boreham Wood in the FA Trophy looked to have backfired when Leon Hunter scored in the 53rd minute. The cavalry, in the form of Jon Main and Danny Kedwell, were then introduced and it was the latter who levelled before Luis Cumbers won the tie with a goal in the third minute of added time.

13th December 1975

More than 8,000 fans saw Southern League champions Wimbledon bow out of the FA Cup, beaten 2-0 by Fourth Division Brentford. Roger Johnson's double before the break put the Bees in control and despite buzzing around the visitors' goal in the second period, the Dons could find no way past their former stopper Paul Priddy. 'We have seen better Southern League sides down here this season,' a clearly frustrated Allen Batsford was quoted as saying at the end.

13th December 1998

Fresh from beating champions Arsenal and knocking Chelsea out of the League Cup, the Dons claimed the scalp of Liverpool as they moved up into the Premier League's top eight. A goal from Robbie Earle and penalty save by Neil Sullivan combined to ensure a 1-0 win over the mighty Reds. 'My lads just love playing against the big clubs and they deserve all they get at present,' manager Joe Kinnear said. 'European football is within our grasp, and I hope we can maintain our form.'

14th December 1974

First-half goals from Ian Cooke and Mick Mahon meant the Dons made it through to the third round of the FA Cup for the first time in their history by beating Southern League rivals Kettering Town 2-0 in front of nearly 6,000 fans at Plough Lane. 'Wimbledon? That's where they play tennis, isn't it?' Jimmy Adamson, the boss of First Division Burnley, quipped when he heard news of the third-round draw the following Monday.

14th December 1993

Neal Ardley's shoot-out penalty finally ended two hours of mounting tension as the Dons advanced into the League Cup quarter-finals at the expense of Liverpool. 'We were magnificent,' manager Joe Kinnear said. 'To concede a goal in the 93rd minute was a devastating body blow but once again we showed the resilience and character we have at this club. Now I don't see why we should not go all the way to Wembley.'

15th December 1984

The lowest league crowd at Ninian Park for 51 years – just 2,976 – looked on as the Dons' 3-1 win sent Cardiff to the bottom of the Second Division table. Striker Stewart Evans plundered a two-goal haul and Kevin Gage wrapped up the points with a solo effort midway through the second half. 'It was very satisfying to win away at last,' manager Dave Bassett said. 'We've played better on other occasions and come away with nothing, so it was good to wrap up three points.'

15th December 2007

Terry Brown set his sights on winning the FA Trophy after his men brushed aside the challenge of Conference South side Maidenhead United. Second-half goals from Marcus Gayle and Antony Howard were enough to see the Ryman Premier League Dons advance. 'We had enough chances to have won by four or five,' the manager commented. 'I honestly feel this side is capable of beating anyone. I see no reason why we should not go to Wembley for the final.'

16th December 1961

Former Dulwich Hamlet star Les Brown grabbed four in a dream debut as the rampant Dons put six unanswered goals past Oxford City in an Isthmian League game at the White House ground. Club chairman Sydney Black had promised the team a night out in London if the England amateur international scored a hat-trick and he was as good as his word taking the side to a restaurant before they headed on to a nightclub in the West End.

16th December 2001

Five hundred fans representing more than 80 clubs travelled to Selhurst Park to protest against the Dons' proposed move to Milton Keynes. Chris Willmott netted a 66th-minute winner against Nottingham Forest on a day when the on-field action seemed rather less important than football politics. Meanwhile, two former sports ministers – Tony Banks and Kate Hoey – were among 70 MPs who signed a House of Commons motion against the move tabled by Wimbledon MP Roger Casale.

17th December 2005

Despite Dave Sargent scoring from the spot, the Ryman League Dons bowed out of the FA Trophy, beaten 3-2 by Conference South high-fliers St Albans. 'I'm never happy when we lose but we can take a lot from that performance,' manager Dave Anderson reflected afterwards. 'It was a cup tie that had everything – goals, penalty appeals, near misses and passion.'

17th December 2011

The Dons were made to pay for poor finishing as they went down 1-0 to Rotherham United in a League Two match played at the Don Valley Stadium in Sheffield. Luke Moore missed an open goal in the first minute and Jack Midson fluffed two relatively easy chances after the break. The full cost of those misses was evident in the 78th minute when Lewis Grabban chased a long ball down the left and pulled a pass back inside for Sam Wood to fire home off the inside of a post.

18th December 1987

John Fashanu's 12th goal of the season was enough for the Dons to beat Norwich City and move up into seventh place in the First Division table. 'When I agreed to coach Wimbledon at the start of the season, I was under the impression that Fashanu was just a big, strong forward who liked to put himself about a bit,' England number two Don Howe said. 'But he is improving all the time, so much so that I would not rule him out of the England picture.'

18th December 1993

Days after recreating the Dambusters' fly-past in celebration of a victory over Liverpool in the League Cup, the Dons returned to Selhurst Park to record a Premier League win over a Sheffield United side including ex-Dons Kevin Gage, Glyn Hodges and Alan Cork. Goals from Warren Barton and Dean Holdsworth saw the surprisingly blunt Blades beaten 2-0. 'Four days ago, I was involved in a penalty shoot-out, today I hardly touched the ball,' goalkeeper Hans Segers reflected.

19th December 1953

Fielding future England cricket coach Mickey Stewart at inside-forward, the Dons won their FA Amateur Cup first-round tie at Stevenage Town. Although there were only around 1,000 spectators at Broadhall Way, many were visiting fans, waving blue and white balloons. Jack Cammell gave Wimbledon an early lead before the team went on to record a 3-1 victory.

19th December 1964

Controversially dropped, Eddie Reynolds marked his Southern League comeback with a hat-trick in the 7-1 win over Ashford Town that silenced his critics and vindicated those who had campaigned for his return. With Paul Hodges missing a penalty and two other goals being disallowed, Wimbledon could well have had double figures as the hosts kept the Ashford goal under siege almost throughout the 90 minutes.

20th December 1986

After successive victories over Manchester United, Chelsea and Sheffield Wednesday, the Dons were brought down to earth as they lost 3-0 at league leaders Everton and a furious Dave Bassett kept his team locked in the dressing room for an hour afterwards. 'Everton gave us a footballing lesson,' centre-back Brian Gayle admitted later. 'We were left chasing the ball and we ended up in a bit of a daze because of their ability to switch the play around.'

20th December 2008

Two goals from Danny Kedwell and another from Jon Main allowed the Dons to complete a Conference South double over Newport. 'Today's win has hopefully set us up for a fabulous Christmas,' a delighted manager Terry Brown commented. 'We desperately needed a good win here at Kingsmeadow to go into the festive period in good form. It was important to keep a clean sheet as I feel we will always score a goal or two.'

21st December 1968

Goals from Ian Cooke, Eddie Bailham and Roy Law allowed the Dons to beat local rivals Guildford City 3-1 and move up to third in the Southern League Premier Division table. Making just his sixth first-team start, teenage goalkeeper Dickie Guy had another good game between the posts. He was to remain the club's number one for the next nine seasons.

21st December 1985

Eight bookings, two red cards, a penalty miss and five goals added up to a wonderful afternoon of pre-Christmas entertainment at Plough Lane. Responding to their manager's call for more goals, the Dons gained emphatic revenge for a heavy defeat in Yorkshire back in August by beating Sheffield United 5-0. 'That was the best we have played all season,' midfielder Ian Holloway commented. 'Even if they had not had two players sent off, we were well on top.'

22nd December 1934

A late train meant a delayed start to the Dons' Isthmian League match at floodlightless Loakes Park and with the light already fairly gloomy due to fog, it was agreed to play 35 minutes each way. After a scrappy and goalless first half, the teams turned round without leaving the field and Wycombe quickly took the lead before Eric Turner levelled. It was almost completely dark as the match ended in a 1-1 draw.

22nd December 1997

Shady Far Eastern betting syndicates were blamed as the Dons' Premier League match with Arsenal was abandoned early in the second half after the lights went out. Commenting on the third floodlight failure of the Premier League season, managing director Sam Hammam said, 'This shouldn't be happening. Once was bad enough, the second wasn't pretty, and this is getting near a disaster. Unless we stop it there will be shame on the game. We are all embarrassed by it.'

23rd December 2000

A red card for Rob Gier failed to stop the Dons' fine run of away performances in the First Division as Terry Burton's men beat Tranmere Rovers 4-0 at Prenton Park. Goals from Trond Andersen, Mark Williams and a Jason Euell double meant the ten men ran out as comfortable winners leaving the manager enthusing, 'I'm delighted. If we can go on and reach the play-offs, it will be a fantastic achievement.'

23rd December 2006

Despite being reduced to ten men late in the second half, an 86th-minute Lewis Cook free kick was enough for the Dons to secure a 1-0 Ryman Premier League win at Heybridge Swifts. 'Fair play to Lewis because it was a great finish,' manager Dave Anderson commented. 'To win after having Chris [Gell] sent off makes it more special. We needed it as we are mid-table and we have got to push on towards the play-offs in the new year.'

24th December 1979

A thrilling FA Cup replay at Fratton Park finished level at 3-3 meaning a second replay between the Dons and Portsmouth. The visitors had come back from 2-0 and 3-2 down to level when, during extra time, the PA announcer informed the crowd that the last Christmas Eve ferry for the Isle of Wight was about to leave. No one moved as the action switched from end to end before Wimbledon won the right to stage the third meeting following a post-match coin toss.

24th December 1983

An end-to-end Christmas Eve Third Division local derby against Brentford was settled in the Dons' favour with just minutes to go when Alan Cork fired home the winner to make the final score 4-3. 'I couldn't have asked for any more at this stage of the season,' beamed manager Dave Bassett. 'Halfway through the campaign and we're well placed for a shot at promotion in the new year.'

25th December 1934

Young Lesley Smith produced a scintillating display on the right wing as the Dons beat Woking 5-1 on Christmas morning. Centre-forward Jack Lock feasted on his crosses to grab a hat-trick as Wimbledon kept up their pursuit of the Isthmian League title. But the following day, the Cards took revenge with a 1-0 win in the return fixture at Kingfield.

25th December 1952

Nearly 4,000 fans turned out on Christmas morning for an eagerly awaited clash with Isthmian League newcomers Bromley. The visitors went ahead early on but a Wimbledon side fielding three reserves should have equalised when Harry Stannard was fouled only for Jack Wallis to miss the subsequent penalty. The half-back made amends with 20 minutes left when he levelled the scores to send both sets of supporters home for their turkey dinner reasonably happy.

26th December 1963

A bumper Boxing Day crowd witnessed one of the greatest fightbacks in the Dons' history as Les Henley's men came from 3-0 down at the break to beat bitter rivals Tooting with almost the last kick of the game. Transformed after the break, Eddie Reynolds scored twice and then Roy Law levelled from the spot before Brian Keats broke the Terrors' hearts with a winner deep into injury time.

26th December 2009

Four goals in the first half an hour put the Dons in complete control of their Blue Square Premier Boxing Day encounter with Hayes & Yeading at Kingsmeadow. 'This was a nice Christmas present from the boys,' manager Terry Brown said after his side had completed a 5-0 win. 'They started really strongly and won every tackle – and every time we went forward, we looked like scoring.'

27th December 1976

Billy Holmes was the star man as Wimbledon ended Barry Fry's Hillingdon Borough's ten-game unbeaten run at the Leas Stadium in west London. The striker's bold running and powerful shooting caused mayhem in the home defence as he set up Roger Connell to volley home the first and then supplied the corner from which Jeff Bryant added the second. The 2-0 victory kept the Dons on course for their third successive Southern League title.

27th December 2003

Unbeaten all season in the Combined Counties League, the Dons rounded off 2003 in style by firing seven goals past Raynes Park Vale to delight the 3,903 fans at Kingsmeadow. 'It was real team performance,' said hat-trick hero Kevin Cooper. 'We all looked after ourselves properly over the Christmas period and we could not wait to get out there in front of what we knew would be a bumper crowd.'

28th December 1987

Second-half goals from Alan Cork, Dennis Wise and Vinnie Jones saw Wimbledon beat Arsenal for the first time as they moved up into the First Division's top six. Describing the win as a 'famous victory', manager Bobby Gould was asked by the press about the prospect of his high-flying team playing in Europe the following season. 'Everyone tipped us for relegation a few months ago but the possibility is not too outrageous,' he commented.

28th December 2015

Tom Elliott was a revelation as he terrorised the Exeter defence for over an hour in helping the Dons to record their first League Two win since 31 October. The powerful forward headed home Barry Fuller's 17th-minute cross and it was 2-0 on the half-hour as a long ball forward was lifted home by Lyle Taylor. 'Four points and two clean sheets in the last few days has been brilliant,' manager Neal Ardley said. 'Now we have got to kick on.'

29th December 1951

With both Freddie Gauntlett and Arthur Maggs registering hat-tricks, the Dons were able to beat Metropolitan League side Skyways with embarrassing ease in the Surrey Senior Cup at Plough Lane. Forced into several late changes meaning several of the team played out of position, the visiting club secretary apologised that his side had not put up a better fight as they went down 8-1. 'We expected a tousing and we got it,' he said.

29th December 2012

Neal Ardley pulled no punches after his team suffered a brutal 3-0 defeat at the hands of Oxford United, a sixth game without a win. 'I have defended the players in the past, but I am not going to defend them after that,' the manager said. 'There are too many players here with weak mentalities. We are bottom of the table for a reason, and I need the players to show a little courage. Not one player did what we asked them before the game.'

30th December 1989

A late goal from substitute Alan Cork was enough for the Dons to secure a 2-2 draw with Manchester United at Plough Lane. 'He has to be the player of the decade for Wimbledon,' manager Bobby Gould said of the striker. 'He has been here through thick and thin and you can always rely on him to pull something special out of the bag.'

30th December 1995

Two goals from Robbie Earle and another from Dean Holdsworth silenced a Highbury crowd of 37,640 as the Dons beat Arsenal 3-1. It capped a highly satisfactory four days for struggling Wimbledon as they had won at Chelsea on Boxing Day. 'We said it at the time, but no one listened that when our 18-man injury list started to clear up we would be all right,' manager Joe Kinnear told reporters.

31st December 1977

The Dons went down 3-1 to runaway Fourth Division leaders Watford meaning the Football League newcomers would begin 1978 in the bottom four. 'We should have scored while we were on top in the first half,' manager Allen Batsford reflected ruefully. A disastrous trip to Swansea followed before the man who had overseen so much Southern League success resigned.

31st December 1988

The Dons ended a remarkable year with their biggest top-flight win to date, 4-0 over Luton Town at Plough Lane. One man who was not impressed was Spurs manager Terry Venables. 'Wimbledon and teams that play like them are killing the greatest game in the world,' he wrote in a newspaper column. 'I could take an average non-league player and within a week turn him into the type of player who could hold a first-team place at Wimbledon. Who wants that?'